PATCHES OF TIME

LINDA HALPIN

PUBLISHING COMPANY

ACKNOWLEDGEMENTS

It is with much gratitude that I wish to thank those who so generously gave of their talent and expertise:

Buffalo and Erie County Historical Society
Chemung County Historical Society
Chitra Publications
Horseheads Historical Society
Jeannette Keyser
Nebraska State Historical Society
Oldest Wooden Schoolhouse

Quilt Digest Press
Marjorie Rosser
Phyllis and Dana Scutt
Stearns Technical Textiles Company
Jean and Leroy Weaver
Winterthur Museum
Judith Youngman

Jeanne and Gene Wilber

with special thanks to...

Steve Appel for his care and precision in photography
The RCW graphic design group, Lynn Balassone and Pamela Jo Cardone,
for translating my sketches into clear and precise graphics
Tom Wilber for his research and technical advise
Mark and Rebecca Wilber for their unending support and enthusiasm

and to my family, without whom I could not have undertaken this project.

CREDITS

Cover - Schoolhouse Revisited 92" x 97"
Owned by Benjamin Youngman
Made by Judith Youngman
Quilted by Lola McCarty

Photography by Stephen J. Appel Photography, Vestal, New York
unless otherwise credited

Patches of Time©
© 1991 by Linda Halpin
Rebecca C. Wilber Publishing Company
RR#3, Old Post Lane
Columbia Cross Roads, Pennsylvania 16914-9535
717-549-3331

ISBN 0-9627646-1-2

Contents

"... for life isn't given to us by the yard length.
It comes in bits and pieces... small patches of time...
and out of them we must each fashion our own quilt of life.
And just like a quilt
no two are exactly alike, and rarely perfect."

Grandma's Devotional
by Theo Eson
Quilter's Newsletter
November, 1973

Survival By Any Means...
Log Cabins and Soddies

...a symbol of an expanding America. Built around a central fireplace, shown by the red central square in the quilt block, although sometimes yellow was used as the center to depict a candle left in the window, beckoning home weary farmers after a long day in the fields, or welcoming strangers passing through. The light half of the block represented the glow provided by the flame, the dark half the shadows.

Not all early Americans lived in log cabins. The first English colonists in North America were not familiar with houses of logs. They lived in shelters made of brush and bark until they could build frame houses like those they had known in England. Like their English counterparts, those first homes had thatched roofs, but colonists soon discovered that wood was more plentiful than reed or straw, and soon replaced thatch with wood. It was colonists from Sweden who first built log cabins when they settled the Delaware Valley in 1638. Other settlers from forest-laden homelands soon followed. The Germans built log homes in Pennsylvania around 1710, followed by the Scotch-Irish in the Appalachian highlands circa 1720. By the Revolutionary War, log cabins were widespread among the settlers along the western frontier.

Although they required few tools, they were not easy to build. Logs had to be chinked (filled in-between spaces) with moss, clay, or mud. Unable to afford glass, some settlers covered window openings with animal skins or greased paper. Doors usually hung on leather hinges. Most log cabins were one story, with one or two rooms. Some had a loft for sleeping and storage. All contained a fireplace. Essential to survival, it was kept burning night and day, providing heat, light, and a means of cooking.

By the 1850's, the log cabin had made its way into the repertoire of quiltmaking patterns. While there is evidence that the mosaic-like arrangement of strips around a central square existed centuries prior to this (a falcon mummy, found in an Egyptian tomb dating to about 500 BC, and now in the Rosicrucian Egyptian Museum in San Jose, California, contains

Constructed by John Hendy, 1789, in Elmira, New York. Collection of the Chemung County Historical Society, Elmira, New York.

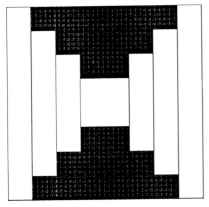

Courthouse Steps Variation

wrappings arranged in what we now call the Log Cabin, Courthouse Step Variation[1]) it took Westward Expansion to translate the log cabin into a quilt block representation. As Americans began moving out West, the log cabin became the symbol for the American spirit.

As with log homes built upon a foundation of stone, log cabin quilt blocks were built upon a foundation of muslin or other cotton fabric. If wadding (batting) was in short supply, this extra layer of fabric eliminated the need for the added warmth provided by an interlining; and without wadding, quilting was not necessary, making log cabin quilts a faster alternative when the warmth of an extra bed covering was required.

Log cabin quilts contained their share of "hidden meaning." With blocks that were visually divided into light and dark halves diagonally, a variety of patterns were formed when blocks were arranged just so. An arrangement of concentric squares radiating from the center of the quilt was named "Barn Raising," depicting the community cooperation that was essential to survival in newly settled territories. Arranged in a diagonal stripe formation, the "Straight Furrows" told of the intimate link to the land that could spell life or death.

A black center in a "Courthouse Steps" arrangement of "logs" symbolized the judge presiding over hall of justice, while a black center in the more traditional Log Cabin arrangement was said to identify the house displaying such a quilt as a station in the Underground Railroad. In Cajun country, a log cabin quilt on a clothesline meant an invitation to a barn-raising.

Yet not all settlers were fortunate enough to be able to build log cabins. The Depression of the 1830's, followed by the Gold Rush of the 1840's and

As stated in The Homestead Act of 1862, any person over 21, who was the head of a family, and either a citizen or an alien who intended to become a citizen, could obtain the title to 160 acres (65 hectares) of public land if he or she lived on the land for five years and improved it. Or, the settler could pay $1.25 per acre in place of the residence requirement.

Mrs. Clarence Carr recalled of her Dawson County sod house, "My mother was always throwing flower seed up on our roof; they would bloom out in damp weather." [2]

Dugout near McCook, Nebraska, 1890's, Solomon D. Butcher Collection / Nebraska State Historical Society, Lincoln, Nebraska

Matilda Coler who grew up in a soddy in western Kansas told her granddaughter that her sod house was warmer in winter and cooler in summer than her later frame house, but she had to stretch a muslin ceiling to catch the falling insects which lived in the sod roof. [3]

"The real economy of a household is shown in the art of gathering all leftovers, so that nothing is wasted. I mean leftovers of time as well as material. Nothing should be thrown away as long as the possibility remains of putting it to use, as meager as it may be; and however large the family may be, every member of it should keep busy earning his money or saving money...In reference to this, patchwork is a good means of saving. It is naturally a crazy waste of time to tear cloth to pieces in order to arrange it anew into fantastic patterns; but a large family may be maintained on insignificant things and a few shillings may be saved through the use of curtain and clothing scraps."

"The American Frugal Housewife" by Lydia Maria Child, 31st edition, 1845

the Homestead Act of 1862 brought settlers in droves over the prairies. The Civil War, too, played a large role in encouraging people to move out West and begin anew. By 1900, almost 150,000 claims for 20 million acres of land had been filed. The prairies were amazingly barren of the trees so familiar in the East. Settlers were forced to find new materials with which to build their homes, and the one thing the prairie had plenty of was grasslands.

Soddies were built on the flat lands. Special plows, or sod cutters, were used to slice strips of sod which were then cut into blocks one foot wide, two feet long, four inches thick, and weighing fifty pounds each. Laid grass side down, side by side, walls were formed that were two feet thick. Wooden frames for doors and windows were formed from brush, and set in place. Sod 'bricks' were set in place, and filled in around. Three weeks, one acre, and ninety tons later, an average one room 16' x 20' soddy was constructed.

Sometimes the tools or work power weren't available for such construction, in which case, caves were dug into a hillside, providing necessary shelter from the elements. Dugouts were not without their drawbacks. Occasionally, a cow grazing on the grasslands was known to wander unknowingly onto the roof of someone's dugout, only to come crashing down on the family within. Although seemingly crude, dugouts and soddies were cool in the summer, warm in the winter, fireproof ... vital in a land where flaming Indian arrows or a raging prairie fire were a constant threat. But they were dark, damp, and heavy rains could cause an indoor mud slide in a matter of minutes.

Inventive sometimes to the point of exhaustion, women made the best of the situation, plastering the interior walls of their earthen homes with newspaper (a source of reading entertainment for all within), cheesecloth, or muslin in an effort to retain the dirt and detain the vermin.

By the end of the century, patterns such as Log Cabin and Dugout had become testaments to the ingenuity of the American spirit. Today, Log Cabin remains a favorite, providing quiltmakers with a pattern format that results in the dynamics of modern art, while retaining the purism of recycling at its best.

Quilting, despite the intricate turn it sometimes takes, has always fallen under the category of "plain work," as opposed to the "fancy work" of embroidery, lacemaking, etc. An 1877 guide to fancy work includes, begrudgingly, a mention of patchwork in its pages, describing both the English method of piecing and the quilt-as-you-go method of construction:

"Patchwork:

Although this work seems to come more under the head of plain than fancy needlework, this little book would scarcely be complete were all reference to it omitted. It is generally our first work and our last...the schoolgirl's little fingers setting their first crowded or straggling stitches of appalling length in patchwork squares, while the old woman, who can no longer conquer the intricacies of fine work, will still make patchwork quilts for coming generations.

Where any scope is given to fancy in patchwork, the pieces should be basted over stiff card, or still better, pieces of tin, and sewed over and over, the card being then removed. Some run the pieces together, some sew them on the sewing-machine, but the old-fashioned overstitch will ever be the best for patchwork.

It is a great improvement upon the huge and unwieldy quilting-frames of the days of our grandmothers, to make the patchwork for a quilt in bound squares. Each one is lined, first with wadding, then with calico quilted neatly, and bound with strips of calico. These squares being then sewed together, the quilt is complete. (This is) much more acceptable than when they must all be quilted together in a huge frame."

Ladies' Guide To Needle Work,
Embroidery, Etc.
being a complete guide to all types of
Ladies' Fancy Work
by S. Annie Frost
1877

What makes this quilt so unusual is the method of construction. While the Log Cabin traditionally is a block pattern built on a base block, the pieced blocks are then usually joined into a quilt top before being joined to a backing. This particular quilt was put together in a "quilt as you go" method, each block joined to its backing, then joined together to make the whole quilt. While usually thought of as a 1970's-and-beyond method of construction, "quilt as you go" was the suggested method of choice in an 1877 Ladies' Guide To Needle Work.[5]

Made of calicos c. 1860-80, these blocks used the backing fabric as the foundation upon which they were built, thus eliminating the additional weight of a batting and separate backing.

The foundation blocks alternate a red with a black fabric of the same print. Attaching a gingham square to the wrong side of the center of each foundation block, logs (strips) of fabric were added by hand until the entire foundation was covered.

By positioning the gingham square in the center, the first log of fabric was placed right sides together, raw edges even with the gingham. Stitched along one edge, through all three layers, the log was then pressed open, thereby concealing the just-constructed seam. A second log was then positioned along the next edge of the gingham square in the same manner, thus concealing the end of log #1 as well as this edge of the gingham square. Logs were continually added in this stitch-and-press method, in clockwise rotation, until the foundation block was completely covered.

Blocks were then placed right sides together and seamed, forming a quilt. The raw seams on the quilt's back were then covered by appliquéing 1/2" wide strips of a red-on-blue sprigged fabric over the seams. 3/8" wide brown print binding was then machine-stitched to the edges, and hand-stitched in place.

Lightweight and portable, this block-by-block method of construction is ideal for a quick-to-finish scrap quilt that requires neither quilting nor tying.

Quilt Sizes:
finished block: 7 1/2" square
centers: 1 1/2" square
logs: 3/4" wide
4 logs per side

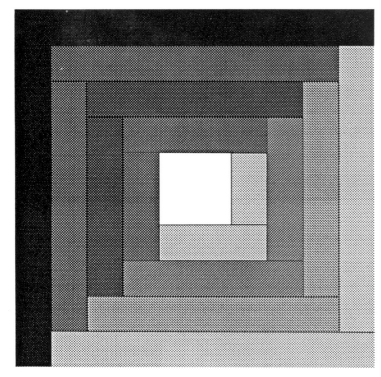

size	dimensions*	# of blocks	layout
crib:	45" x 60"	48	6 x 8
single:	75" x 105"	140	10 x 14
full/queen:	90" x 105"	168	12 x 14

*All dimensions are ample enough to tuck quilt in around pillow.

CONSTRUCTION OF QUILT-AS-YOU-GO LOG CABIN:

YARDAGE:
44" wide fabric (narrower fabric requires greater yardage): Yardage is given for making a back with squares that alternate two fabrics, seams covered with a third fabric, edges bound with a forth fabric.

If desired, the backing could be one fabric (simply total the listed yardages together*), or they could be a variety of fabrics, utilizing fabrics you already have on hand.

crib:
center squares	1/4 yd.
*backing	1 1/4 yd. EACH of 2 fabrics
*seam covering	1 yd.
*outer binding	5/8 yd.
*(total: 4 1/8 yd)	

single:
center squares	1/2 yd.
*backing	3 1/4 yds. EACH of 2 fabrics
*seam covering	2 1/2 yds.
*outer binding	7/8 yd.
*(total: 9 7/8 yds)	

full/queen:
center squares	1/2 yd.
*backing	4 yds. EACH of 2 fabrics
*seam covering	2 1/2 yds.
*outer binding	1 yd.
*(total: 11 1/2 yds.)	

Logs:
assorted scraps, variety of light, medium, and dark fabrics. Be aware that the value of fabrics (light-medium-dark) is relative. Next to one fabric, a fabric may appear light, while in combination with another fabric, it may seem dark. This is what makes antique scrap quilts so intriguing. The same fabric may appear in both the 'light' and 'dark' positions in different locations of the quilt, depending on what fabrics surround it. Don't be afraid to experiment. It will add a dash of excitement to your quilt.

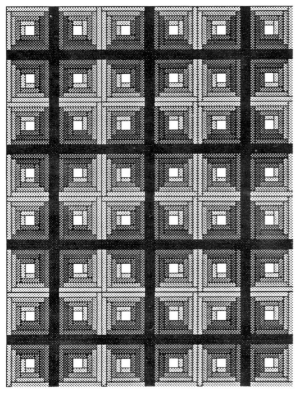

Crib quilt (6 x 8 block layout)

measurements include 1/4" seams

CRIB

backing: (24) 8" squares EACH of 2 fabrics
centers: (48) 2" squares
logs: strips 1 1/4" wide
of assorted fabrics
seam covering: (1) 32" square
(See *Bias Binding:* page 104
cut 650" bias 1 1/2" wide)
outer binding: (1) 22" square
(See *Bias Binding:* page 104
cut 220" bias 2" wide)

SINGLE

backing: (70) 8" squares EACH of 2 fabrics
centers: (140) 2" squares
logs: strips 1 1/4" wide
of assorted fabrics
seam covering: (2) 40" squares
(See *Bias Binding:* page 104
cut 2000" bias 1 1/2" wide)
outer binding: (1) 28" square
(See *Bias Binding:* page 104
cut 370" bias 2" wide)

FULL / QUEEN

backing: (84) 8" squares EACH of 2 fabrics
centers: (168) 2" squares
logs: strips 1 1/4" wide
of assorted fabrics
seam covering: (2) 43" squares
(See *Bias Binding:* page 104
cut 2450" bias 1 1/2" wide)
outer binding: (1) 30" square
(See *Bias Binding:* page 104
cut 400" bias 2" wide)

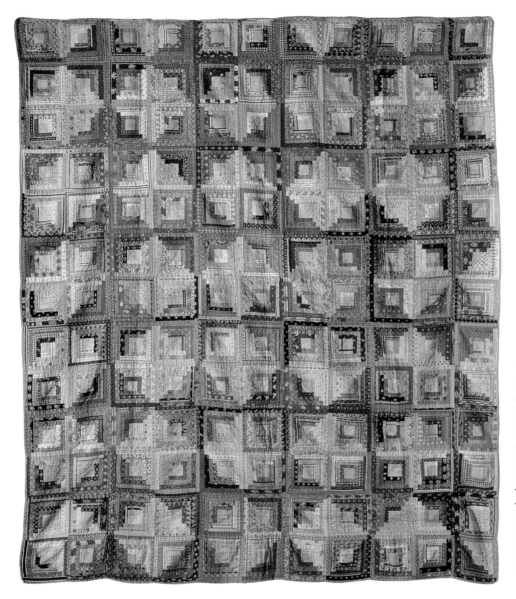

68 3/4" x 81 1/4" Made c. 1860-80, this log cabin quilt contains an array of fabrics typical of the day. Constructed in a quilt-as-you-go method, individual squares, seen in detail below, used squares of the backing fabric (below, right) as their foundation. Resulting seams were then covered over with strips of fabric appliquéd in place. Collection of the Chemung County Historical Society, Elmira, New York.

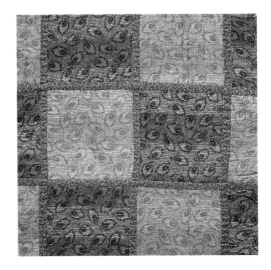

Construction:

(Use 1/4" seams throughout)

1. Fold foundation/backing block in quarters diagonally, corner to corner, and press.

2. Fold the center square in quarters in the same manner.

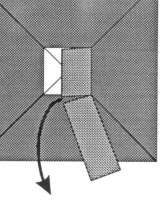

3. Lay the foundation/backing block WRONG SIDE UP. Position the center square on the foundation/backing block, RIGHT SIDE UP, aligning creases so as to center the square. Pin in place.

4. To attach logs, lay the first log (strip of light fabric) right sides together, raw edge even with the right hand edge of the center square. Trim off segment of log strip's length that is in excess of the center square.

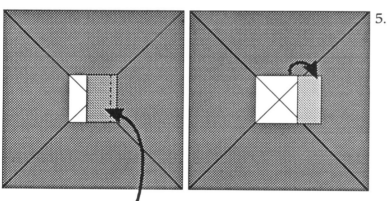

5. Stitch 1/4" from aligned edge, through all 3 layers of cloth. Press log open, thereby concealing the seam you just made.

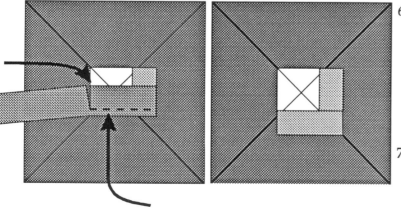

6. Attach the next log in the same fashion, using the same light fabric. Position this log along the bottom of the center square, beginning at the edge of the first log, and trim off the log strip's length that is in excess of the center square.

7. Stitch 1/4" from this aligned edge through all 3 layers of cloth. Press log open.

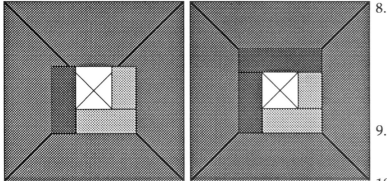

8. Attach the next log, this time using a dark fabric, positioning this log along the left hand edge of the center square, beginning at the edge of the previous log, and trimming off the log strip's length that is in excess of the center square.

9. Stitch 1/4" from this aligned edge through all 3 layers of cloth. Press log open.

10. Attach the next log, using the same dark fabric, positioning in the same fashion, along the top of the center square. Stitch and press.

Notice that logs are added in clockwise rotation around the center square, first using a light strip for the first two logs (in the 3:00 and 6:00 positions), followed by a dark strip for the next two logs (in the 9:00 and 12:00 positions)

Additional logs are added in the same rotation, using a new light and new dark strip in each rotation, until a total of four logs have been added to each side of the center square. This will completely cover the foundation/backing block.

"In using spool-cotton, thread the needle with the end which comes off first, and not the end where you break it off. This often prevents kinks."

The American Woman's Home
(A Guide to Women in How To Keep a Home)
by Catharine E. Beecher
and Harriet Beecher Stowe
1869
p. 354 [6]

HINT:

Hand Piecing: *Knots will be concealed if you begin stitching on the log side of the unit. As the log is opened, the knot is covered.*

Machine Piecing: *For the neatest back, do not backtack. Instead, lock your stitches by beginning and ending stitching with 3" long tails. Each time you remove the unit from the machine to prepare for the next step, pull the tail from the back up through to the log side. Tie off in a double knot. Clip off excess tail. Press log open. This will cover the knots. Every time you wonder about all the extra work in hiding the knots, remember that you are saving time by stitching the seams by machine, and that you will not have to quilt the bed covering when you are done!*

For the best accuracy, press with a dry iron after the addition of each log.

For speed and continuity, you may want to attach the first log to several blocks, then the second log to several blocks, etc. This will complete several blocks at a time in assembly line fashion.

JOINING BLOCKS:

Lay blocks out to achieve desired arrangement. Blocks will then be joined to form rows, with rows then being joined to form the entire quilt.

1. Press 1 1/2" wide bias strip in half, wrong sides together.

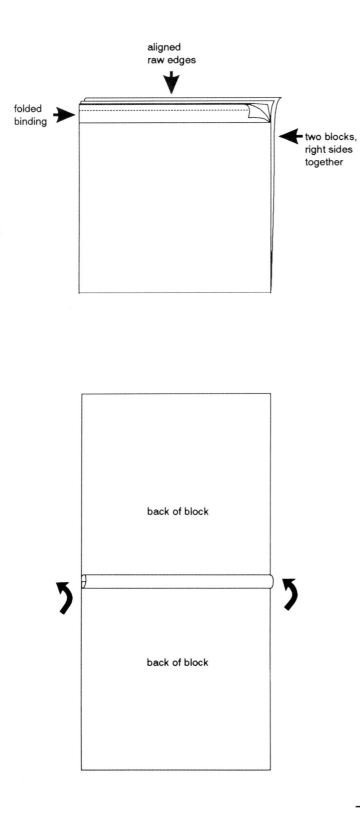

2. Place two log cabin blocks right sides together, raw edges even. Pin. Place an 8" length of folded bias strip along the pinned edge, aligning all raw edges. Stitch through all layers with a 1/4" seam.

3. Press open the log cabin blocks. On the back, press all layers of the seam allowance to one side, covering seam with the folded bias strip.

4. Blindstitch folded bias strip in place, taking care that stitches do not go through to the front of the quilt.

5. Complete rows by adding blocks in the same fashion, concealing seams as you go.

6. Join rows in the same manner, matching block seams as you stitch. Blindstitch bias to conceal seams. The quilt is now ready to bind around the edges.

7. Using the 2" wide bias strips, bind the raw edges around the outer edge of the quilt. (see chapter on *Finishing Finesse*.)

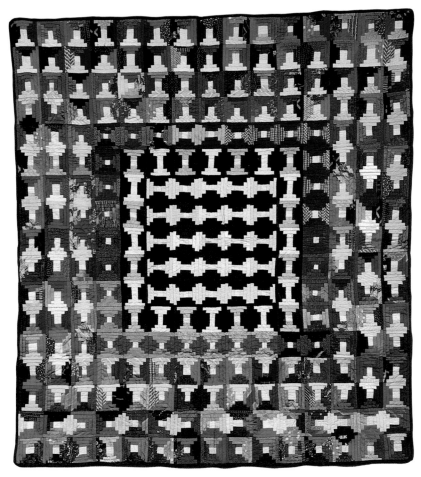

Courthouse Steps: 50 1/2" x 57 1/4" Made by Nellie Anger Miller, 1895, age sixteen. Constructed in similar fashion to the traditional log cabin block, strips of fabric are arranged around a central square to form a block of desired size. This particular quilt uses a crazy quilt as its backing. Collection of the Buffalo and Erie County Historical Society.

Straight Furrows 68" x 78 3/4" Taking its name from the diagonal rows formed by the light and dark arrangement of the log cabin squares, this 1892 quilt contains 4,420 pieces. Collection of the Buffalo and Erie County Historical Society.

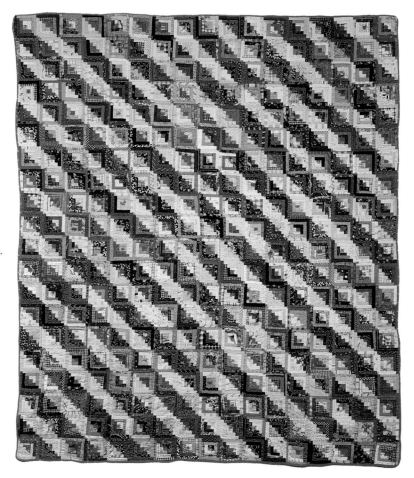

1897 saw many country schoolhouses as one room operations. Children from school #10, in Veteran, New York pose for this class portrait. Collection of the Horseheads Historical Society.

A Schoolhouse Revisted

Schools have long been an important part of American culture. 129 years before Independence, the Massachusetts Colony passed (in 1647) the first law requiring every town with at least 50 families to provide elementary schools for all children. Wealthy families continued to educate their children in a variety of ways, ranging from private schools (or "dame schools," often run by widowed ladies in their homes), to tutors, to boarding schools overseas. By the 1700's, private secondary schools called academies opened in many colonies, teaching bookkeeping, navigation, English, Latin, and other practical subjects geared primarily to the education of boys. Some academies admitted girls, while a few were for girls only. In the early 1800's, states gave communities authority to collect property taxes to pay for schools, not only making schooling more readily available to all economic groups, but also giving women an occupation option other than marriage.

Schoolhouses were, for the most part, one-room structures in which all students learned together. It wasn't until 1847, in Quincy, Massachusetts, that students were divided into grade levels and taught separately. Public schools served as a center of community activity throughout most of the 1800's. Spelling bees, town meetings, and other special events were held in the school. As the population began moving out West to settle new lands, or seek the riches of gold, towns began sprouting up along the frontier, and teachers were in short supply. Teaching was one of the few socially acceptable reasons a single woman could partake in the expansionist movement.

Education for young girls consisted of subjects that would better prepare them for their roles as a wife and homemaker. From 1799 to 1843, at the Society of Friends Westtown School in Westtown, Pennsylvania, female students, some as young as 10 years of age, spent two weeks out of every six learning and polishing their sewing skills. The subject, an effort to be creative as well as practical, taught neatness, accuracy, careful planning, and patience. Sewing was as much a part of the curriculum as was English, reading, spelling, and simple arithmetic. Many of the skills taught during sew-

1872 Rules for Teachers[1]

1. *Teachers each day will fill lamps, clean chimneys.*
2. *Each teacher will bring a bucket of water and a scuttle of coal for the day's session.*
3. *Make your pens carefully. You may whittle nibs to the individual taste of the pupils.*
4. *Men teachers may take one evening each week for courting purposes, or two evenings a week if they go to church regularly.*
5. *After ten hours in school, the teachers may spend the remaining time reading the Bible or other good books.*
6. *Women teachers who marry or engage in unseemly conduct will be dismissed.*
7. *Every teacher should lay aside from each day's pay a goodly sum of his earnings for his benefit during his declining years so that he will not become a burden on society.*
8. *Any teacher who smokes, uses liquor in any form, frequents pool or public halls or gets shaved in a barber shop will give good reason to suspect his worth, intention, integrity and honesty.*
9. *The teacher who performs his labor faithfully and without fault for five years will be given an increase of twenty-five cents per week in his pay, providing the Board of Education approves.*

ing exercises were executed in the construction of samplers. The primary purpose of early 18th century samplers was to provide practice in working numerals and alphabets. The numerals and letters recorded on these samplers could be copied onto clothing and household linens to identify them. In a period when many linens were hand-woven, replacement was not an easy task, so in order to insure even wear, linens were labeled so they could be used in rotation to insure long life.

By 1830, mass media was making its way into more and more homes. With more and more women learning how to read, a market was created for magazines geared to women and what interested them. Godey's Lady's Book began publishing in 1830, and remained one of the most popular and long-lived ladies' magazines of the day. It contained everything from hand-colored plates illustrating the newest fashions, to stories, songs, poetry, recipes, puzzles, games, household hints, and directions for a variety of needle arts. Obtainable for a subscription rate of $3 per year, women's groups could subscribe at reduced rates by ordering in quantity. While quilting patterns were sometimes illustrated, they were not identified by name, and seldom contained directions. One wonders how, with education only in simple arithmetic, women knew how to devise their own patterns.

In fact, they did know. As stated by quilt historian Ruth Finley, young girls were taught the mysteries of paper folding[2] and cutting long before entering school. What was termed simple arithmetic in the 1800's would astound scholars of today. As late as 1892, a teaching manual for kindergarten teachers, advocated using paper folding as a way to learn shapes, straight lines, parallel lines, angles, and fractions. Not only did children create squares, triangles, rectangles, and diamonds, they knew what they looked like, how they felt, and how they could be used with each other to create more intricate shapes. Evidence that these class plans were indeed put into use is shown in the collection of the Buffalo and Erie County Historical Society, who owns paper folding designs and paper cut-out designs that were part of 1st Buffalo Kindergarten Training Class, 1891-1893.[4]

These lessons were followed by exercises in building a color wheel, mixing of colors, (including

"An excellent test in drawing will be found in a dictation exercise - for example, tell the children to think of a square prism, four inches long, two inches wide, and two inches high, resting on the table, and on a level with the eye. Suppose the prism to be in a direct front view, with an oblong face, in a vertical position. Ask the children to draw the front view."
p. 73 ... Primary Manual Training
Caroline F. Cutler
1892

Answer: The solution to this puzzle depends upon the student understanding the terms presented to them. A square prism is one quarter of a cube. The resulting diagram in answer to the above dictation would be like so:[3]

To the W.H. Blair family of 1888 near Broken Bow, Nebraska, the sewing machine was an important enough part of their household to be included in the family portrait when Solomon D. Butcher came to photograph the life and times of the Nebraska pioneer. Courtesy of the Solomon D. Butcher Collection / Nebraska State Historical Society, Lincoln, Nebraska.

A lock stitch machine was invented by Walter Hunt in the 1830's,[5] but never patented. While Elias Howe patented a more sophisticated model in 1846, Isaac Singer is the one who first sold the machines in quantity. Originally costing $500, Singer developed the installment plan to increase demand, and therefore production, which in turn lowered prices by increasing volume. In 1860, 111,000 machines were sold at $75 each. By 1871, the price had dropped to $25. While zig-zag machines were available commercially as early as the 1870's, they were not a part of the home sewing machine option until the 1950's.

tints, shades, and tones), and lessons on color harmony to a depth that today is often not discussed until college level.

Sewing remained a part of a girl's schooling throughout the 1800's. Given that as many as twelve hours a day were spent sewing just to provide daily household needs, it is no wonder that the advent of the sewing machine was so joyously received. Patented in 1846, the sewing machine was at first extremely expensive. Families would pool together to purchase a machine, rotating it among the owners for use. So important was the sewing machine in a family's possession that it was sometimes included in family portraits, which were in themselves a wondrous bit of new technology. In view of the fact that a dress which took six and one half hours by hand could be made in fifty seven minutes by machine, and a shirt requiring fourteen hours could be constructed in one hour, it is no wonder that the sewing machine was held in such high regard.

While Isaac Singer is not credited with inventing the sewing machine, he is acknowledged to have been a genius at merchandising the new product. Up until this time, it was customary to expect men to operate machines, while women, who were of much more delicate constitutions, could only operate tools. In an effort to overcome this prejudice which threatened to kill his sales,

Singer insisted that salesmen and shopkeepers use their wives to demonstrate the machines, showing that they were "simple enough even for a woman to use." In addition, he recognized that the pillars of the women's community were the ministers' wives. Obtaining the seal of approval of the clergy wives meant future sales in the remainder of the town. In view of this, Singer gave free sewing machines to the wives of ministers. Sales jumped from nearly 3,600 in 1858 to over 127,000 in 1870.

And, lest financing was a problem, Singer instituted the installment plan. For $5 down, and $5 a month, any family could be the proud owner of a new sewing machine.

With less and less time required to tend the home, more and more time was devoted to the education of girls outside the domestic sphere. The schoolhouse became a focal point of a young girl's life. As a pieced quilt design, the Schoolhouse appeared in the last quarter of the 19th century. Called the Log Cabin in the 1890's, it may have referred to the Benjamin Harrison Log Cabin Presidential Campaign of 1888. Also known as Old Kentucky Home, Old Folks at Home, and Lincoln Log Cabin, it wasn't identified as the Little Red Schoolhouse until Ruth Finley called it such in 1929.[6]

With renewed interest in traditional quilt patterns, the schoolhouse has enjoyed revived popularity. Combined with appliqué techniques for narrow stems which allow for charming detailing, the *Schoolhouse Revisited* pays tribute to a favorite pattern.

Variations on the traditional schoolhouse block take the design one step further, with windows sashed, and doors hinged and handled. While seemingly complex, the windows are sashed with strip-piecing shortcuts, while the door trimmings employ appliqué as a change of pace from machine piecing.

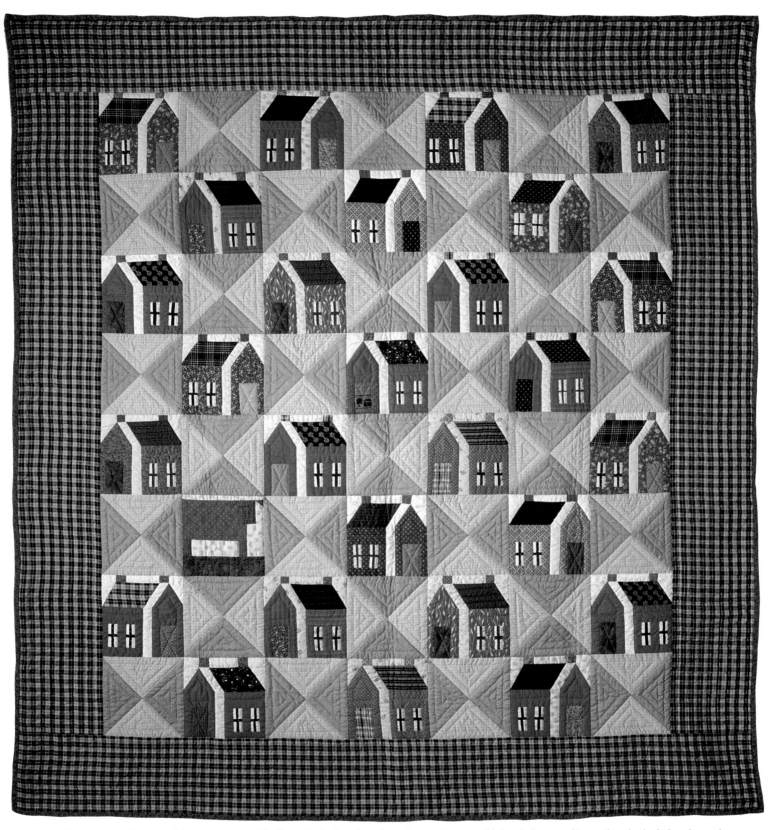

It was felt that to make something perfect would offend God, therefore, in order not to anger higher beings, quilters often included a planned mistake, or "humility block" in their work. Choosing to adapt the Schoolhouse Revisited block in her own fashion, quilt artist Judith Youngman made this quilt for her son Benjamin's college graduation, incorporating a "humility block" with just a touch of whimsy.

For precision machine piecing that builds in a seam allowance "custom-fit" to your sewing machine's presser foot:

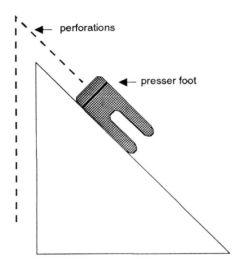

Draw the "finished size" of each shape in the pattern on a sheet of paper, leaving approximately 3/4" between shapes. With an UNTHREADED machine, stitch around each shape, positioning the edge of the presser foot along the edge of the shape, perforating the pattern sheet approximately* 1/4" outside the edge of each shape.

*(The actual distance from the edge of each shape will be the width of your presser foot.)

The "dotted line" will be the size of your template for machine piecing, building in a seam allowance that works on YOUR machine.

Lay translucent plastic template material over the perforated pattern sheet. Draw templates the perforated size. Cut out.

Position on fabric, trace around edges of template, and cut on the pencil line. When you cut the fabric this new size, and align the raw edges of the fabric pieces with the edge of your presser foot, you will end up with finished pieces the size drawn on the original pattern sheet, regardless of the width of your presser foot.

SCHOOLHOUSE REVISITED

Templates are given for 10" blocks. For the look of an antique scrap quilt, schoolhouses may be made of fabrics from your collection. If you prefer a more orderly look to your quilt, all the schoolhouses may be the same. Directions for two different ways to set the blocks together, along with yardage requirements, follow the general directions on the block's construction.

SCHOOLHOUSE REVISITED: 10" BLOCKS

CUTTING
light fabric: sky, door, windows, house sashing
    1 A (sky)
    1 A reversed (Ar) (sky)
    1 C (sky)
    1 E (house sashing)
    1 G (house sashing)
    1 I (door)
    2 N (window panes)
medium fabric: schoolhouse, chimneys
    2 B(chimneys)
    1 D (house)
    2 H (house)
    1 J (house)
    2 K (house)
    1 L (house)
    1 M (house)
dark fabric: roof, window sashing, door hinges, door knob
    1 F (roof)
    1 O (window sashing)
    2 P (window sashing, door hinges, door knob)

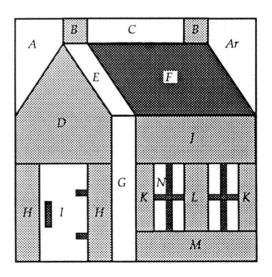

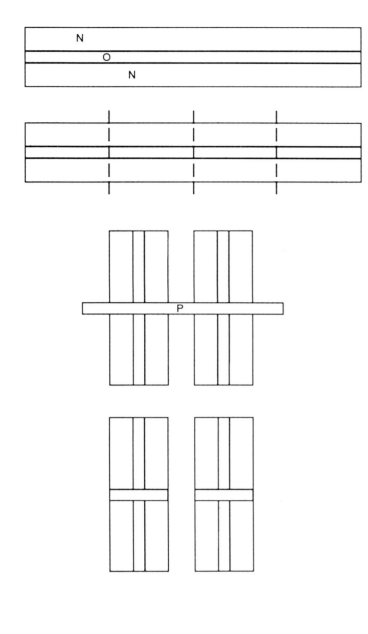

CONSTRUCTION

WINDOWS

1. Place one N right sides together with one O, aligning along one long edge. Position the aligned edge even with the edge of your presser foot. Stitch with a 1/4" seam.

2. Place remaining N piece to the other long edge of O, as in step 1. Stitch, and press. This gives you an N-O-N band.

3. Cut 4 slices, each 1 3/4" long, as shown:

4. To form windows, join slices to one piece P as shown.

    HINT: be sure to align sashes of upper and lower windows.

5. Trim off excess P, resulting in 2 windows. *HINT: or try using a plaid that would allow you to use the lines of the design as the sashing strips and eliminate having to piece them.*

DOOR

1. From the remaining P piece, cut two pieces 1" long and one piece 1 1/2" long.

2. Hinges
    a. Tuck in 1/4" on each 1" piece. Press in half.

    b. Refer to pattern sheet for placement guide.
    c. Stitch to door where shown, with a backstitch.

    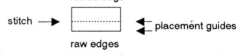

    d. Fold to cover seam allowance. Appliqué folded edges in place. Press.

    e. Repeat with remaining hinge

4. Door knob
    a. Tuck in 1/4" on both ends of the 1 1/2" long piece. It is now 1" long. Press in half, as with hinges.
    b. Apply to door as in steps 3b through 3d.

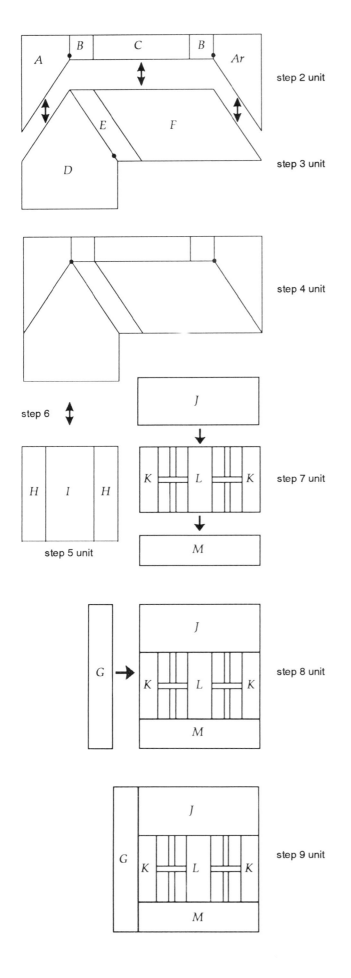

step 2 unit

step 3 unit

step 4 unit

step 6

step 7 unit

step 5 unit

step 8 unit

step 9 unit

HOUSE

1. Join B - C - B.

2. Join A - BCB - Ar. NOTE: Stop stitching a "seam allowance width away" from one end. See dot in illustration.

3. Join D - E - F, again stopping where shown by the dot.

4. Join the step 2 unit to the step 3 unit. Press.
   HINT: To prevent puckers:
   Join A - D, lockstitch at dot
   Join BCB - EF, lockstitching at dots
   Join F - Ar, lockstitch at dot

5. Join H - I - H. Press.

6. Join HIH (door unit) - D (house gable unit). Press.

7. Join K - window - L - window - K. Press.

8. Join J (house above windows) - step 7 unit (windows) - M (house below windows). Press.

9. Join step 8 unit to G (house sashing). Press.

10. Join step 9 unit to rest of block, completing the block. Press.

Blocks may now be set together in the style of your choice. Directions for settings with sashes, as well as with quarter-square triangles follow, with yardages given for three sizes in each style. Feel free to create a schoolhouse keepsake of your own.

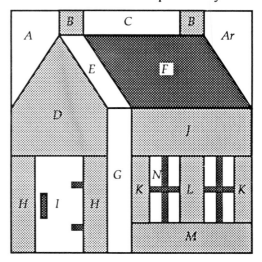

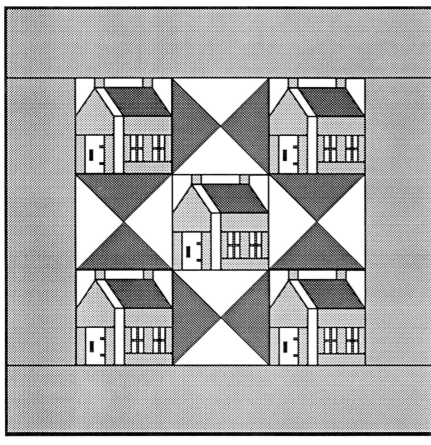

VARIATION #1
set together with quarter square triangles as in quilt on cover

CRIB: 46" X 46"
3 x 3 block layout: 5 houses,
4 quarter square triangles
YARDAGES:*
houses: may be made out of scraps, but
if purchasing fabric
lights: 1/2 yard
mediums: 1/2 yard
darks: 3/8 yard
triangles: 1/2 yard EACH of two fabrics
border: 1 1/2 yards
      cut (2) 8 1/2" x 30 1/2"
      cut (2) 8 1/2" x 46 1/2"
binding: 5/8 yard
      cut (1) 21" square**
backing: 3 yards

SINGLE: 70" X 90"
5 x 7 block layout: 18 houses,
17 quarter square triangles
YARDAGES:*
houses: may be made out of scraps, but
if purchasing fabric
lights: 1 1/2 yards
mediums: 1 1/2 yards
darks: 1 yard
triangles: 1 1/8 yds. EACH of two fabrics
border: 2 1/4 yards
      cut (4) 10 1/2" X 70 1/2"
binding: 7/8 yard
      cut (1) 27" square**
backing: 5 1/4 yards

FULL/QUEEN: 90" X 100"
(cover)
7 x 8 block layout: 28 houses,
28 quarter square triangles
YARDAGES:*
houses: may be made out of scraps, but
if purchasing fabric
lights: 2 yards
mediums: 2 yards
darks: 1 1/2 yards
triangles: 1 3/4 yds. EACH of two fabrics
border: 2 3/4 yards
      cut (2) 10 1/2" x 80 1/2"
      cut (2) 10 1/2" x 90 1/2"
binding: 1 yard
      cut (1) 30" square**
backing: 7 3/4 yards

*measurements include 1/4" seams
**See *Finishing Finesse* for directions on construction of binding

This method allows you to sew, then cut, resulting in two triangles that have already been pieced together. This shortens the construction time considerably, and eliminates the need for you to work with bias edges, assuring better accuracy.

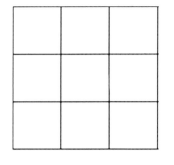

1. Place the two fabrics for triangles right sides together. On the wrong side of the lighter fabric, draw squares as shown.

    squares for all sizes are 11 1/4" square
    crib: draw 2
    single: draw 9
    full/queen: draw 14

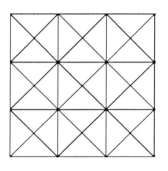

2. Draw diagonal lines, corner to corner, in BOTH directions on EVERY square.

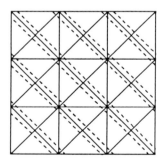

3. Stitch 1/4" on BOTH SIDES of ONE DIAGONAL LINE ONLY in EACH square. Be sure your 1/4" seam is accurate, otherwise the various units used in this block will not go together properly.

4. Press to flatten stitched fabric.

5. Cut on ALL lines drawn. This will result in the following units:

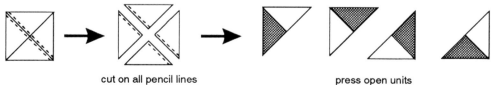

cut on all pencil lines   press open units

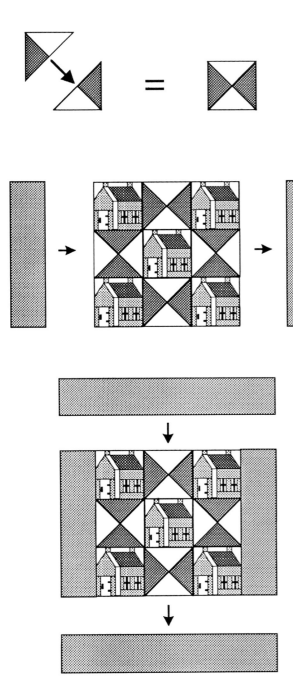

6. Join units as shown, creating quarter square triangles. Construct the following:
   crib: 4 squares
   single: 17 squares (there will be one extra)
   full/queen: 28 squares

7. Lay out blocks, alternating schoolhouse and quarter square triangle blocks in desired arrangement.

8. Join blocks to form quilt top.

9. Add short border strips to sides of quilt. (See *Finishing Finesse* for hints on successful addition of borders)

10. Add long border strips to top and bottom of quilt.

Your quilt top is now complete, ready to be quilted and finished.

HINT: To construct the template for the quarter square technique for any size block, figure out how large the finished unit should be. To construct the template, add 1 1/4" to this measurement. A 10" finished block (as in our quilt), requires an 11 1/4" template.

For each time you draw the template on the fabric, you will end up with two finished squares. Example: the full/queen size needs 28 finished squares...draw the template on the fabric 14 times.

Regardless of the size of the square, the 'magic number' for the quarter square triangle technique is 1 1/4"

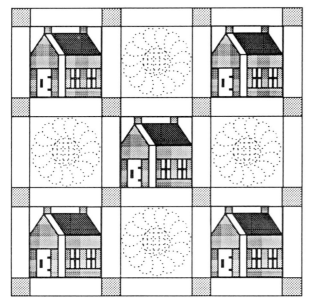

VARIATION #2
set with sashing and alternate plain squares

CRIB: 40" X 40"

3 x 3 block layout:
5 houses, 4 plain squares

YARDAGES:

houses: may be made out of scraps, but if purchasing fabric
lights: 1/2 yard
mediums: 1/2 yard
darks: 3/8 yard
alternate plain squares: 1/2 yard - cut (4) 10 1/2" square
sashes: 5/8 yard - cut (24) 3" x 10 1/2"
intersecting squares: 1/4 yard - cut (16) 3" square
binding: cut (1) 21" square*
backing: 1 1/2 yards

SINGLE: 65" X 90"

5 x 7 block layout:
18 houses, 17 plain squares

YARDAGES:

houses: may be made out of scraps, but if purchasing fabric
lights: 1 1/2 yards
mediums: 1 1/2 yards
darks: 1 yard
alternate plain squares: 1 3/4 yds - cut (17) 10 1/2" sq.
sashes: 2 yards - cut (82) 3" x 10 1/2"
intersecting squares: 1/2 yard - cut (48) 3" square
binding: 7/8 yard - cut (1) 27" square*
backing: 5 1/4 yards

FULL/QUEEN: 90" X 115"

7 x 9 block layout:
32 houses, 31 plain squares

YARDAGES:

houses: may be made out of scraps, but if purchasing fabric
lights: 2 1/4 yards
mediums: 2 1/4 yards
darks: 1 1/2 yards
alternate plain squares: 3 yards - cut (31) 10 1/2" square
sashes: 3 1/2 yds. - cut (142) 3" x 10 1/2 "
intersecting squares: 3/4 yard - cut (80) 3" square
binding: 1 yard - cut (1) 30" square*
backing: 8 1/4 yards

*See *Finishing Finesse* for directions on construction of binding.

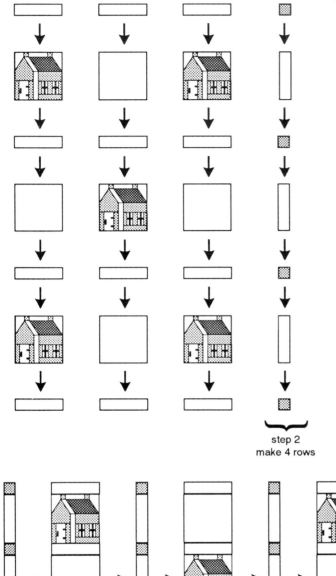

step 2
make 4 rows

SETTING HINT:
When joining blocks with sashing, a good visual propor-
tion is to cut lattice strips 1/5 - 1/4 the width of the block
you are setting together. For our 10" schoolhouse block,
that would mean sashing 2" - 2 1/2" wide.

1. For ease in joining quilt top, join blocks to sashing to form the required number of rows.

2. Join sashing to intersecting squares to form strips that go between the rows of houses.

3. Join all rows to form the quilt top.

Alternate squares make a great place to do quilting. Several quilting patterns may be located in the chapter *Stitch by Stitch, the Texture of Quilting.*

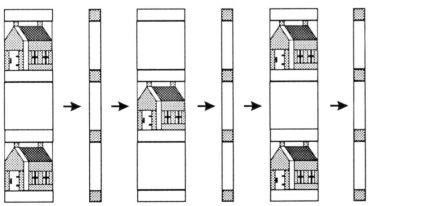

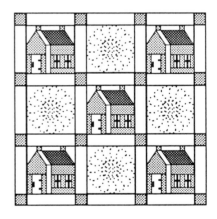

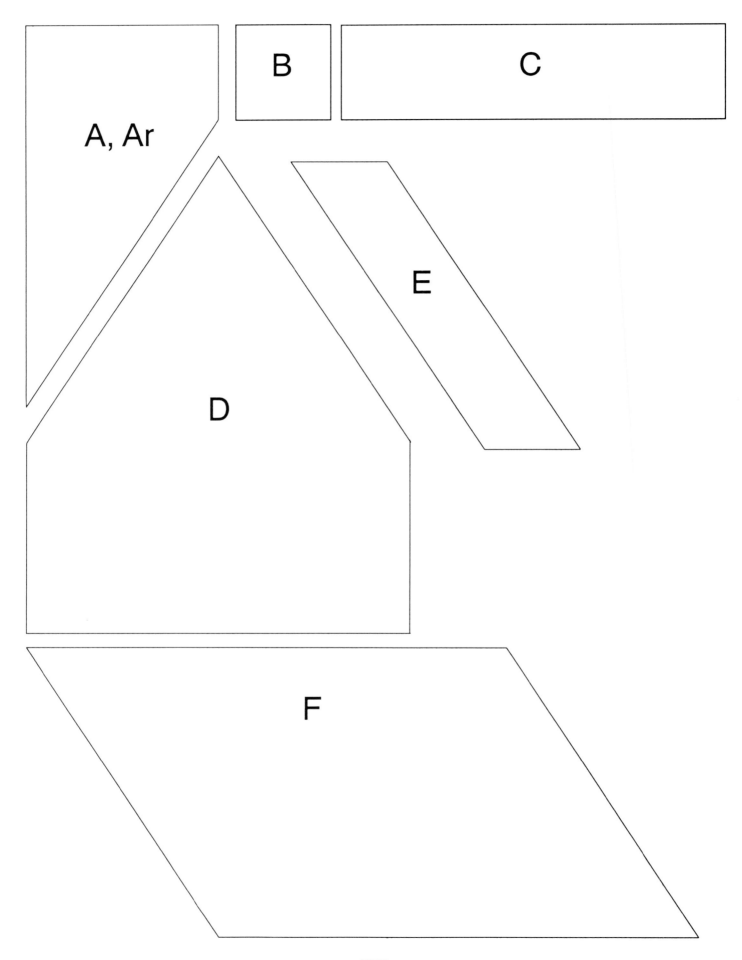

A, Ar

B

C

D

E

F

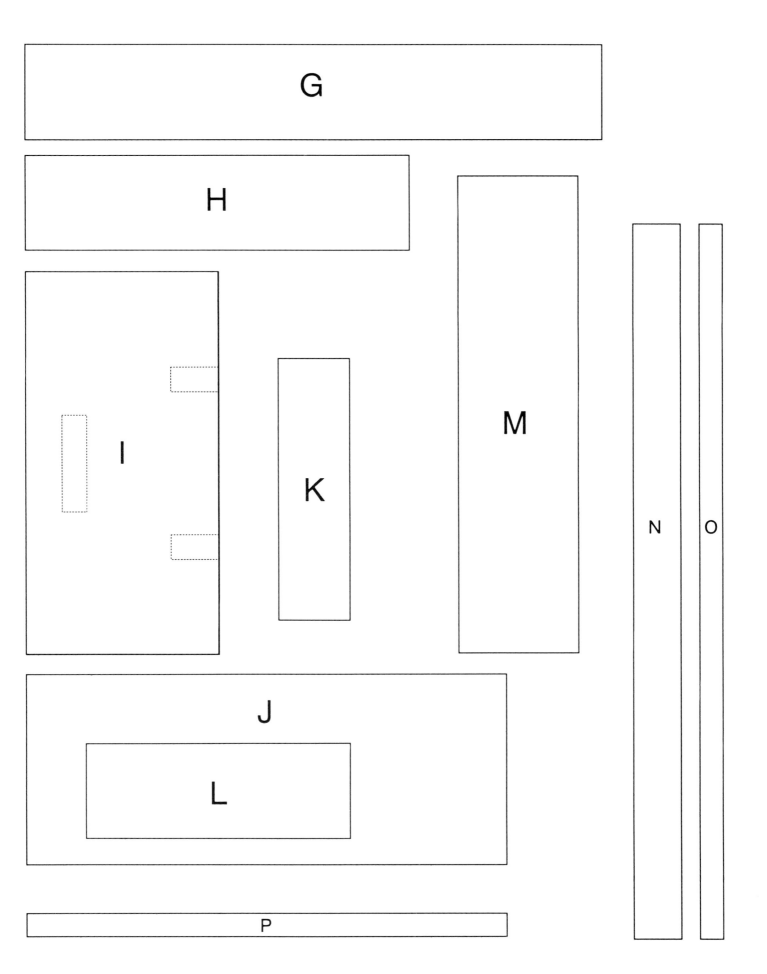

Bear's Paw 50" x 50" What sets this Bear's Paw quilt apart from all the rest is the sawtooth edging which graces the surrounding border. Long strips which are specially cut are folded and appliquéd in place so as to form triangles in a fraction of the time it would take to piece them. It is a nice change of pace from the rhythm of machine piecing used to construct the quilt top, and lends elegance to a favorite traditional pattern. Made by Marjorie Rosser, Williamsport, Pennsylvania, quilted by Mildred Cavanaugh.

THE WILDERNESS AROUND US...
THE BEAR'S PAW

Most quilt historians would agree that the Bear's Paw is a pattern with a frontier-inspired name, taking inspiration from the early days of America when pioneers had to stake their claim against nature. While the design is wide-spread, it has been known by many names over the years. To those in western Pennsylvania and Ohio, it was the Bear's Paw; yet to the Quakers of Philadelphia it was called the Hand of Friendship; while quilters on Long Island called it Duck's Foot in the Mud.

Part of the reason for such discrepancies is the lack of printed patterns prior to the 1880's.[1] Many patterns were spread by word-of-mouth, shared among family and friends, or purchased from traveling salesmen. Poor memories for a given name, a salesman's romanticizing of a name to insure a sale, as well as a quilter's desire to name her own design, have all contributed to the wealth of names attributed to many patterns.

In 1889, for the first time, quilters were treated to the availability of a mail order pattern source in *Diagrams of Quilt, Sofa and Pincushion Patterns*, a catalog of patterns for sale from the Ladies' Art Company in St. Louis, Missouri. By 1922, a special volume containing exclusively quilting patterns joined the Ladies' Art Company offerings, joining the ranks of mail order catalogs with Sears, Roebuck and Company, and Butterick. Pattern #357, "bear's foot," was one of over five hundred designs that were by 1928 available for 15¢ each (2 for 25¢). Each came in an envelope with a colored cardboard diagram of the design, showing how many pieces of each shape were needed, and all included the paper templates for the making of the block. Those preferring to follow a cloth block as a guide could order finished 15" blocks (60¢ each / or 12 for $7) or complete quilts (ranging from $25 to $45 each).

Calicos, in addition to patterns, were also available from such mail order sources as Montgomery Ward, Sears, Roebuck and Company, and Ladies' Art Company. Available in widths from 24" - 36", oiled calico (today known as glazed chintz) vied in popularity with ginghams (light-to-medium weight washable cotton, woven in solids, stripes, checks, or plaids).

One of the things which makes this quilt so special is the attention to detail in the sawtoothing on the border. Edging such as this, in which a strip of fabric is periodically slashed, with cut edges folded back into jagged peaks and appliqued to the edge of the quilt, appears on quilts made in the early 1800's, and is rarely seen after 1850.[2] The sawtooth motif itself began appearing on clothing and embroidered samplers at the turn of the 19th century. Inspired by the detailed paintings of the Dutch artist Van Dyck, clothing designers used this form of embellishment as a cheaper alternative to lace.[3] Whether the quilts influenced the samplers, or the samplers influenced the quilts is not known. In any case, the technique used to create the edging is ingenious indeed, accomplishing a seemingly complex task with clever simplicity.

Strips of fabric are laid along the edge of the border, slashed at prescribed intervals, then folded back to form triangular peaks. With the folded edges appliquéd in place, a sawtooth edge is completed in a fraction of the time it would take to cut and sew the myriad of triangles it would take to piece the same effect.

BEAR'S PAW QUILT TOP: 2 FABRICS

Directions are given for 4 sizes, with the Bear's Paw block for the crib quilt scaled down to be in better proportion to the smaller size of the overall quilt. To eliminate piecing of long border pieces, cut borders first out of the length of the yardgoods.

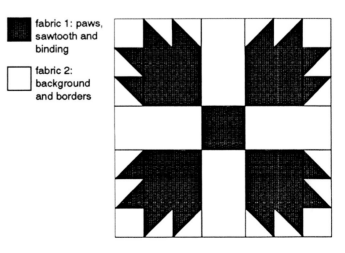

fabric 1: paws, sawtooth and binding

fabric 2: background and borders

CRIB (46" x 46")
FINISHED BLOCK SIZE 8 3/4"
NUMBER OF BLOCKS 9

YARDAGE
fabric 1	1 1/2 yds.
fabric 2	2 1/2 yds.
backing	3 yds.

CUTTING
(measurements include seams)

fabric 1	sawtoothing	(8) 1 1/2" x 48"**
	binding	(1) 20" square
	"C"	(36) 2 3/4" square
	"D"	(9) 2 1/2" square
fabric 2	border	(4) 5" x 48"**
		(4) 9 1/4" square
		(8) edging blocks
		(4) corner blocks
	"A"	(36) 1 5/8" square
	"E"	(36) 2 1/2" x 3 7/8"

* to cut "B" units - see construction steps 1 - 6 pg 36
** cut slightly longer than needed to give margin for error

SINGLE (73" x 88")
FINISHED BLOCK SIZE 10 1/2"
NUMBER OF BLOCKS 20

YARDAGE
fabric 1	3 yds.
fabric 2	5 1/2 yds.
backing	5 1/4 yds.

CUTTING
(measurements include seams)

fabric 1	sawtoothing	(4) 1 7/8" x 75"**
		(4) 1 7/8" x 90"**
	binding	(1) 26" square
	"C"	(80) 3 1/4" square
	"D"	(20) 2 3/4" square
fabric 2	border	(2) 7 3/8" x 75"**
		(2) 7 3/8" x 90"**
		(12) 11" square
		(14) edging blocks
		(4) corner blocks
	"A"	(80) 1 7/8" square
	"E"	(80) 2 3/4" x 4 5/8"

* to cut "B" units - see construction steps 1 - 6 pg 36
** cut slightly longer than needed to give margin for error

FULL (88" x 88")
FINISHED BLOCK SIZE 10 1/2"
NUMBER OF BLOCKS 25

YARDAGE
fabric 1	3 1/2 yds.
fabric 2	6 1/2 yds.
backing	7 3/4 yds.

CUTTING
(measurements include seams)

fabric 1	sawtoothing	(8) 1 7/8" x 90"**
	binding	(1) 28" square
	"C"	(100) 3 1/4" square
	"D"	(25) 2 3/4" square
fabric 2	border	(4) 7 3/8" x 90"**
		(16) 11" square
		(16) edging blocks
		(4) corner blocks
	"A"	(100) 1 7/8" square
	"E"	(100) 2 3/4" x 4 5/8"

* to cut "B" units - see construction steps 1 - 6 pg 36
** cut slightly longer than needed to give margin for error

QUEEN (88" x 103")
FINISHED BLOCK SIZE 10 1/2"
NUMBER OF BLOCKS 30

YARDAGE
fabric 1	4 yds.
fabric 2	7 1/2 yds.
backing	7 3/4 yds.

CUTTING
(measurements include seams)

fabric 1	sawtoothing	(4) 1 7/8" x 90"**
		(4) 1 7/8" x 105"**
	binding	(1) 29" square
	"C"	(120) 3 1/4" square
	"D"	(30) 2 3/4" square
fabric 2	border	(2) 7 3/8" x 90"**
		(2) 7 3/8" x 105"**
		(20) 11" square
		(18) edging blocks
		(4) corner blocks
	"A"	(120) 1 7/8" square
	"E"	(120) 2 3/4" x 4 5/8"

* to cut "B" units - see construction steps 1 - 6 pg 36
** cut slightly longer than needed to give margin for error

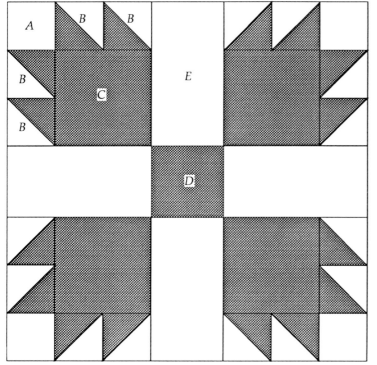

units needed per block:
4 A = small square
16 B = half square triangles
4 C = large square
1 D = medium square in center
4 E = rectangle

TO CONSTRUCT HALF SQUARE TRIANGLES

(B in finished block):

This method allows you to sew, then cut, resulting in two triangles that have already been pieced together. This eliminates the need for you to work with bias edges, assuring better accuracy.

1. Place fabrics 1 and 2 rights sides together. On the wrong side of the lighter fabric, draw the required number of squares as shown, with sides touching.

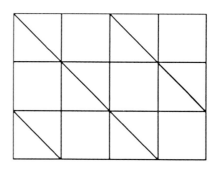

crib quilt: squares are 2" square
             draw 72
single quilt: squares are 2 1/4" square
             draw 160
full quilt: squares are 2 1/4" square
             draw 200
queen size: squares are 2 1/4" square
             draw 240
       (measurements include seams)

2. Draw a diagonal line through every other square.

3. Draw a diagonal line through the empty squares in the OPPOSITE direction.

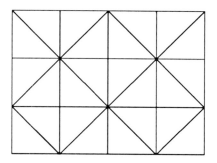

4. Stitch 1/4" on BOTH SIDES of all DIAGONAL lines. Be sure your 1/4" seam is accurate, otherwise the various units used in this block will not go together properly.

TIME SAVING HINT: Stitch in the direction shown by the arrows, pivoting at the outer boundaries of the fabric. When you have completed the path on one side of all diagonals, reverse your path to complete stitching on the other side of all diagonals.

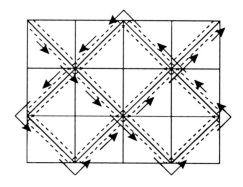

5. Cut on ALL lines.

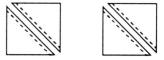

HINT: To construct the template for this technique for any size block, figure out how large the finished half-square triangle unit should be. To construct template, add 7/8" to this measurement. A 1 1/8" finished pieced square (as in the crib quilt) requires a square template 2" for this technique. For a 3" finished pieced square, the template would be 3 7/8". (Regardless of the size of the square, the "magic number" to use for this technique is 7/8"). For each time you draw the template on the fabric, you will end up with two finished squares.

6. Press resulting units open, pressing both layers of seam to darker fabric.

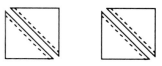

HINT: Place unit on ironing board light side down, darker fabric on top. Lift up dark fabric, and press open. Pressing in this manner will automatically result in both layers of the seam allowance being pressed to the darker fabric.

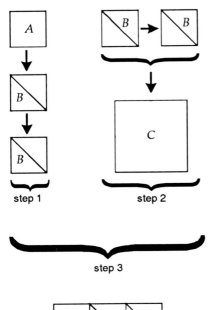

step 1

step 2

step 3

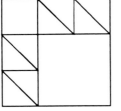

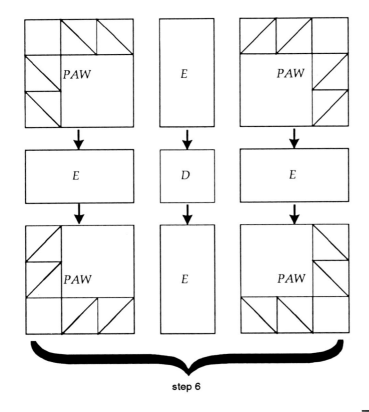

step 6

CONSTRUCTING A BEAR'S PAW BLOCK:

1. Join A-B-B. Make 4. Press.

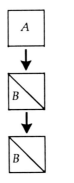

2. Join B-B-C. Make 4. Press.

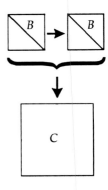

3. Join A-B-B to B-B-C to make a Bear's Paw. Make 4. Press.

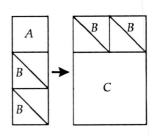

4. Join paw-E-paw. Make 2. Press.

5. Join E-D-E. Make 1. Press.

6. Join (paw-E-paw) to (E-D-E) to (paw-E-paw). Press. Block is complete.

The number of required Bear's Paw blocks for each size is as follows:

crib	9
single	20
full	25
queen	30

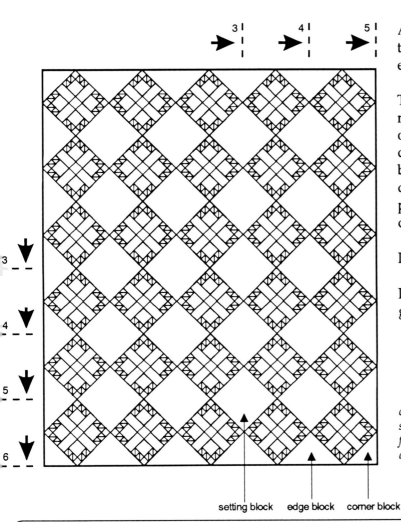

Alternate blocks in this quilt are left unpieced so as to give you the opportunity to show off quilting elegance.

To assist you in joining the Bear's Paws and alternate blocks, use this blueprint as a guideline. Mark off your desired size on this overall diagram. The quilt top is constructed much like an individual block, in rows, only this time the rows are on the diagonal. Use this diagram as a guide to join the pieced blocks, setting blocks, edge blocks, and corner blocks in the proper sequence.

Press seams to one side as you construct each row.

Press seams to one side as you join the rows together.

crib: 3 x 3
single: 4 x 5
full: 5 x 5
queen: 5 x 6

setting block   edge block   corner block

To construct templates for "edging blocks" and "corner blocks":

1   Draw a line the "desired block size" long.
     Crib: 8 3/4"   all other sizes: 10 1/2"

2.   At the endpoints, draw a line at a 90 degree angle to create square corners. Draw these lines the "desired block size" long. This completes sides two and three of the square.

3.   Connect the endpoints of sides two and three. Measure to be sure side four is the correct length and the corners are square.

4.   To obtain template for "edging blocks", draw a diagonal line, corner to corner, through the square. One of the resulting triangles is your template. Place this diagonal line on the straight of grain when tracing template on fabric. Remember to add seam allowances when cutting fabric.

5.   To obtain template for "corner blocks", draw diagonals in both directions, corner to corner, through the square. One of the resulting triangles is your template. Place the edges created by the diagonal lines on the straight grain when tracing template on fabric. Remember to add seam allowances when cutting fabric.

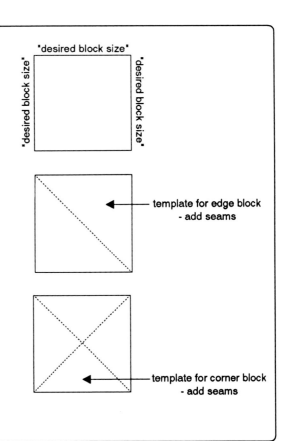

"desired block size"

"desired block size"

"desired block size"

"desired block size"

template for edge block
- add seams

template for corner block
- add seams

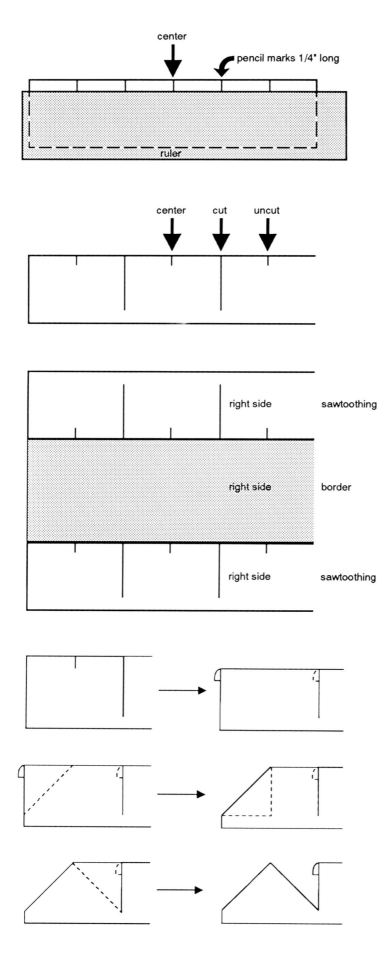

BORDER CONSTRUCTION:
Sawtooth Borders

1. Fold all strips in half to find the center of length. Mark with a pin.

2. On the wrong side of the sawtooth strips: lay a plexiglass ruler (ex: C-Thru) on fabric so all but 1/4" is covered.
    crib: 1 1/4" covered
    single-full-queen: 1 5/8" covered

3. Beginning at center, working toward both ends, mark fabric every (crib: 1"), (single-full-queen: 1 3/8") with a 1/4" long pencil mark. You may have some excess at the ends due to the extra length you allowed as a margin of error.

4. Now, on the first mark on EACH SIDE of the center, cut fabric (crib: 1 1/4") (single-full-queen: 1 3/8") long. Repeat with EVERY OTHER mark as shown.

    NOTE: Cut will stop 1/4" from edge of strip.

5. Pin a sawtooth strip to each long edge of the border strips, matching the centers, right sides up, uncut edges of sawtooth strip even with the raw edge of the background fabric strip.

6. Baste, by hand or machine, the sawtooth strips to the background strips within the seam allowance area near the raw edge. This eliminates several pins.

7. To form the sawteeth:
    The UNCUT marks are the peaks. The CUT marks are folded back to form the valleys.

a. first fold: at peak, fold under raw edge 1/4" to form seam allowance at the top of the peak. *NOTE: as pencil mark is 1/4" long, this is easy to do.*

b. second fold: tuck under the left flap, folding from peak to valley.
c. third fold: repeat with the right flap.

This forms a sawtooth. Appliqué in place. Continue until all sawteeth have been appliquéd in place. Take care that all peaks and valleys align with the peaks and valleys across from them.

See chapter on *Finishing Finesse* for directions on cutting a continuous strip of binding, and edge finishes.

76" x 90" Feathered wreath quilting and sawtooth edging bestow an air of traditional beauty to Judith Youngman's 1990 rendition of the Bear's Paw. Quilted by Lola McCarty.

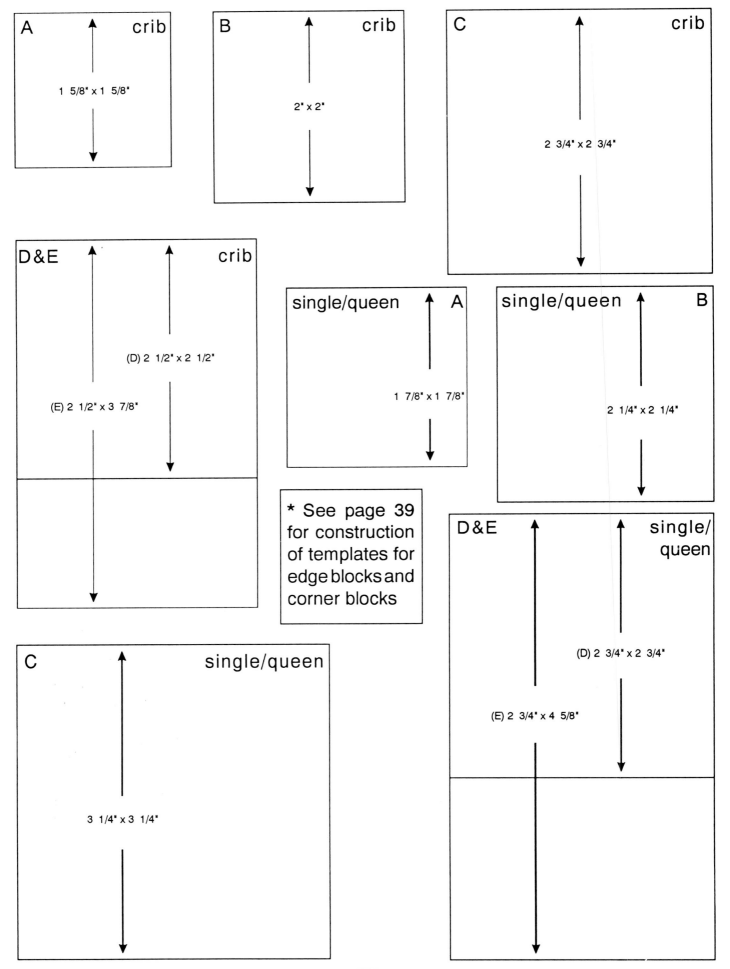

A   crib

1 5/8" x 1 5/8"

B   crib

2" x 2"

C   crib

2 3/4" x 2 3/4"

D&E   crib

(D) 2 1/2" x 2 1/2"

(E) 2 1/2" x 3 7/8"

single/queen   A

1 7/8" x 1 7/8"

single/queen   B

2 1/4" x 2 1/4"

* See page 39 for construction of templates for edge blocks and corner blocks

C   single/queen

3 1/4" x 3 1/4"

D&E   single/queen

(D) 2 3/4" x 2 3/4"

(E) 2 3/4" x 4 5/8"

THE ROSE...
A FLOWER OF HOPES AND DREAMS

One of the most important possessions a family could own was a Bible. Because of it, they learned to read. In it, they not only recorded their family's history, but sought comfort and guidance in their daily lives. The Rose of Sharon, taking its name from the Old Testament, tells of undying love.

"I am the rose of Sharon
and the lily of the valley.
As the lily among the thorns
So is my love among the daughters;
As the apple tree among the trees of the wood
So is my beloved among the sons."

Song of Solomon, Old Testament

The Ohio Rose, one of the many various rose patterns in quiltmaking, was often the pattern of choice for a Bridal quilt. Courtesy of Stearns Technical Textiles Company.

Annie Soule wrote that, as a child in Kansas in the 1850's, she and her sister slept in the cabin's loft, often to wake up on winter mornings with several inches of snow on the quilt. (Jean Dubois)

In the early days of our country, prior to the luxury of central heating, a warm winter home was only 55 degrees. The desire for a great number of quilts was not a matter of pride, it was a matter of survival. This was a time when as many as twelve hours every day might be spent in some form of needlework. Not only were quilts homemade, but so were all of the items needed for everyday living: bed linens, table linens, curtains, clothing, (including underwear), not to mention in some cases the fabric, used for these items. Food was home grown, which meant gardens were tended, livestock was fed, animals were butchered, food was preserved, candles and soap were homemade, as well as everything else needed to run a household.

Children, boys as well as girls, began training for the duties of survival at an early age. Custom was that a bride was expected to begin her new household with a baker's dozen quilts. Due to the often freezing temperatures, a lack of quilts could literally be a matter of life and death. To this end, children began sewing as early as three years of age.

While the first twelve quilts increased the stitcher's ever-growing skills, the thirteenth of the baker's dozen was usually made to showcase the bride's most masterful needlework. Begun only after the young woman's engagement, this Bridal Quilt was often laden with the symbols of love.

A young girl spent much of her youth making quilt tops for the day when she would have her own household, building up to a dozen quilt tops for her dowry by the time she became engaged. These years of experience not only gave her a vast store of sewing skills, but a great deal of time to plan the masterpiece quilt that would be known as her bridal quilt. To make a bridal quilt before one became engaged was sure to mean spinsterhood, therefore, the making of a bridal quilt was taken very seriously. It was the quilt given the most care and the best craftsmanship a young girl was capable of.

When they had made the last roll of the quilt (in the frame), married women left the frame and girls began a contest to see who should set the last stitch. She would be the first to take a husband.

Homespun Handicrafts p. 158

It was said that the first dream dreamed under a newly made quilt would come true. Today, in an age when quilts are not commonplace to everyday exist-ence, a piece of wedding cake under a guest's pillow is said to bring on dreams of their love-to-be.

Until the 20th century, the announcement of an engagement was often celebrated by a gathering of friends, each bearing their scrap bag for the joint creation of a friendship quilt. As this practice died down, it was replaced by the gathering of friends bearing household gifts for the bride-to-be, giving rise to today's bridal showers.

In early Christianity, the Rose became the symbol for the Virgin Mary, with rose hips being used to form the rosary upon which one prayed to the Mother of God for forgiveness and piety.[1]

Begun only after the young woman's engagement, the Bridal Quilt was often laden with the symbols of love, particularly the heart, that heretofore was forbidden, lest she might jinx herself into spinsterhood.

Bridal quilt styles varied. White-on-white quilts were in vogue from 1775-1850, in part due the popularity of one-color textured quilts in Europe. They represented the highest quality one could achieve. The finest fabric was reserved for the quilt top, so as to justly show off the skill of the quilter, for while everyone could patch a quilt together, not everyone was capable of quilting well. White-on-white quilts were therefore the height of showman-ship, demonstrating mastery of great skill as a needleworker.

Between 1800 and 1840, the general format of quilt construction changed. Quilts constructed in blocks became popular. They were easier to man-age than quilts consisting of one block the size of the finished quilt, and fit in much better with the life-style of a changing America who was experi-encing industrialization as well as westward ex-pansion.

The first block-style appliqué quilts appear to have been miniature adaptations of the full-sized Chintz Appliqué, or Broderie Perse quilts made up to this time. Motifs were cut from printed fabrics and placed onto a backing to form the arrangement of choice. Stitched onto a full-sized background, they imitated the very expensive printed Indian palampores (full-size bedspreads) first introduced to Europe by spice merchants of the 1600's.

Block-sized bouquets and wreaths of chintz flowers, imitations in a scaled down versions of the medallion format Chintz quilts so popular in both Europe and America, began to appear by the 1840's. It wasn't until after this time that quilters began to "imitate the imitations" by creating their own flow-ers with appliqué as we now think of it. The first appliqué block quilts appear to have been album quilts, that is, quilts whose blocks were a collection of a variety of designs, due in part to the popularity of albums in general during this time in our history. If people had more than two of something, they began a collection, be it buttons, glassware, pressed flowers, or quilt blocks.

As styles changed, block quilts with squares of all one pattern became the style of choice, with appliquéd rose patterns becoming a quick favorite. Grown by the Chinese as early as the third millen-nium B.C., the rose has served as inspiration for

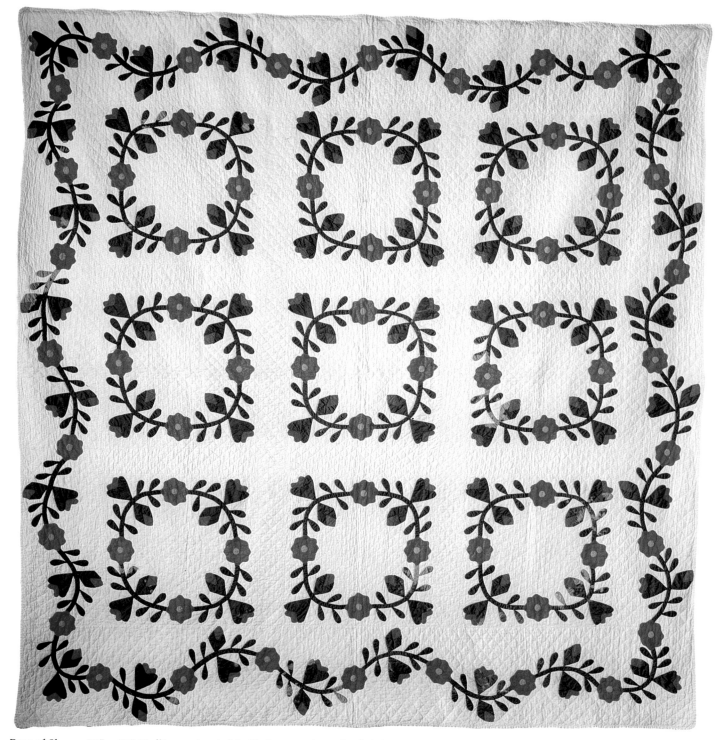

Rose of Sharon 86" x 88" Quilts constructed in blocks were the style of choice from the 1840's on. Owned by Jeannette Keyser, this lovely c. 1850 quilt used turkey red and an overdyed green fabric, popular combinations of the day. A colorfast green was a difficult color to obtain until the use of synthetic dyes after about 1860. Prior to this time, green was obtained by dying the fabric first yellow, then blue (or vice versa, depending on the printer). Problems arose when one color faded or washed out before the other. Such was the case with this quilt when it was washed. The blue, not being colorfast, left the fabric in several areas, causing uneven coloration on much of the quilt. Even so, the overall beauty and craftsmanship of the quilt remain evident to this day.

83" x 83" As was the practice during the Victorian era, women spoke volumes through the use of symbols in their quilts. The hospitality of the pineapple takes center stage in this spectacular mid-19th century quilt believed to have been the Bridal Quilt of Hannah Hess. Made when she was 16, the quilt tells of a young girl's dreams, filled with tulips, the symbol of true love, doves, the symbol of peace, and rose buds, symbol of beauty, purity, and youth. Yet Hannah was not without her faults. She so enjoyed smoking her pipe... but only in the privacy of her own room, never in public. Owned by Hannah's great-grandson and his wife, Leroy and Jean Weaver. Photo courtesy of Chitra Publications.

Due to the many-seeded nature of the fruit, the pomegranate became the symbol for abundance. Not to be confused with the Love Apple, which was the common name for the tomato, (grown in flower gardens for ornamentation, and not popular as a food until after the Civil War), the pomegranate was another popular motif for inclusion in Bridal Quilts. Courtesy of The Stearns Technical Textile Company.

A possible explanation to the brown stains sometimes found on antique quilts may be found in the following bit of advice to housekeepers of the 1860's.

"Modes of Destroying Insects and Vermin: Moths

Airing clothes does not destroy moths, but laying them in a hot sun does. If articles be tightly sewed up in linen when laid away, and fine tobacco put about them, it is a sure protection. This should be done in April."

The American Woman's Home; A Guide to Women in How To Keep a Home
by Catharine E. Beecher and Harriet Beecher Stowe
p. 377
1869[2]

design in every form of decorative art, and quilt-making is no exception. A popular flower in gardens of the day, young girls had ample access to the rose for inspiration in their creation. Almost invariably chosen for the "bride's quilt" of a young girl's trousseau, it has been interpreted in many variations, all of which are based on a built-up rose surrounded by stems, leaves, and buds. It has become the ultimate symbol of romantic love. Because of the great pride taken in these quilts, many have been cherished over the years, helping to insure their survival to the present day.

The construction of Bridal quilts remained a popular custom well after the Civil War. As the greatest expense of constructing any quilt was the padding and backing, the baker's dozen quilts which were such an important part of a bride's trousseau were usually not quilted until after the engagement became official. At this time, quilting bees were held to complete the transformation of quilt tops into quilts, in celebration of the upcoming nuptials.

There is much delightful folklore woven into the use of symbols on bridal quilts. Many of the symbols used so frequently on quilts first came to America from Europe through the Far East during the Crusades.

The tulip, symbol of true love, began in Persia, traveled (as did the actual flower) to Holland, then to America. From the Orient came the symbols of hospitality (the pineapple), abundance (the pomegranate), and the cycle of life (circle or ring).

If a border design was used, in either appliqué or quilting, it was important that it traveled smoothly around the edge of the quilt, unbroken at the corners, for a border that was broken foretold of a life cut short by tragedy. The Hindu peacock promised fertility, while the Tree of Life, bearing the fruits of life eternal, remained a popular subject for many quilts.

In addition to the actual designs used on quilts, much folklore is woven into the usage of quilts. One bit of lore involves a part of the engagement festivities in which, after the women finish quilting, the men join them for a square dance. Upon taking the last quilt out of the frame, a cat was placed in the

The Whig Rose, a popular mid-19th century appliqué pattern, (shown, above) was adapted by gloating women of Democratic persuasion into a pattern combining piecing with appliqué. Transforming the sawtooth edging of the Whig Rose into a pieced diamond arc, the blossom looses its bloom. Being surrounded by the tail feathers of the Democratic symbol, the rooster (shown, below) the pattern was renamed Whig's Defeat. Not having the right to vote did not stop women of the day from having their say.

center of the newly finished quilt, whose edges were held by the unwed members of the group. The cat, then tossed into the air, was said to land closest to the next person to be married. Today, we toss bouquets and garters to the same end.[3]

And perhaps most foreboding of all, was the belief that a girl without a trousseau of quilts would never see her bridal sun.

While the Rose of Sharon became the pattern of choice for symbolizing romantic love, the Whig Rose gained in popularity as a way for women to have their political say in a day when they were yet denied the right to vote.

The Whigs were an active political party in America from 1834 - 1854. Formed in opposition to Andrew Jackson, the Whigs fought to gain a foothold in American politics. When their first successful presidential candidate, William Henry Harrison, died one month after taking office, the Whig party struggled to regain control. Their conviction in the power of compromise managed to at least temporarily unite the eastern capitalists, the western farmers, and for a time, the southern planters. As slavery became an ever increasing concern, a successful compromise was not possible. After the defeat of their staunch leader, Henry Clay, to James Polk in 1844, the Whigs regained temporary control with the 1848 victory of Zachary Taylor, only to fizzle out by 1854 into non-existence. The Whig Rose, most often executed in red and green, was the pattern of choice for Whig loyalists. Defeated time and time again by the Democratic Party, the story of American politics was translated into cloth by quiltmakers of the day. With the rooster as the Democratic symbol (the donkey was not adopted as the Democratic symbol until the end of the 19th century), the victorious party was immortalized in quilting when the Whig Rose, by the addition of petals symbolizing the rooster's tail feathers, became Whig's Defeat.

Whatever the inspiration, patterns influenced by the rose have been beloved throughout time, and remain today some of the most actively sought after.

Whig Rose Quilt Top

Directions are given for 4 sizes. All sizes contain 4 blocks, with the motifs in each size scaled down to be in better proportion to the size of the overall quilt. For ease in construction, go through the pattern, and mark the measurements that apply to the size you are making. Yardages are given for pink sashing and binding for all sizes.

Measurements and Yardage Requirements

	CRIB	SINGLE	QUEEN	KING
Finished Size	41" x 41"	72" x 72"	84" x 84"	97" x 97"
Block Size	15"	25"	28"	33"
# Blocks	4	4	4	4
Yardage:				
background	1 1/2 yds.	5 yds.	5 3/4 yds.	6 1/2 yds.
pink	1 1/2 yds.	3 yds.	3 1/4 yds.	4 1/4 yds.
red	3/4 yd.	1 yd.	1 yd.	1 1/2 yds.
green	1 1/4 yds.	1 3/4 yds.	2 1/4 yds.	2 3/4 yds.
gold	1/4 yd.	1/4 yd.	1/4 yd.	1/4 yd.
backing	1 1/2 yds.	4 1/2 yds.	5 yds.	7 1/2 yds.

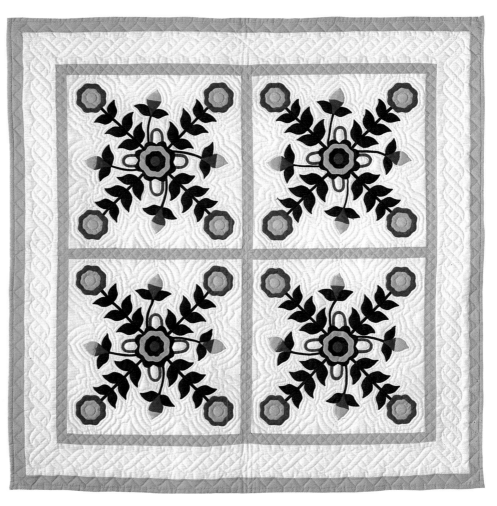

44" x 44" Whether called the Whig Rose, or Rose of Sharon, this multi-layered blossom, complete with buds, is as lovely executed today as were its predecessors a century and a half ago. The appliqué artistry of Marjorie Rosser, complemented by Mildred Cavanaugh's quilting, creates a treasure to cherish.

Whig Rose Crib block section

*As for the stems used throughout the quilt, there is no template given because we will be cutting strips of fabric on the bias and using them to form the stems.

See *How To Make Narrow Even Stems* on page 55 for cutting and construction methods for foolproof stems every time. Dotted lines indicate stem placement. Use diagrams as a guide when marking placement guidelines onto your base blocks.

Whig Rose Single block section

CUTTING FOR A WHIG ROSE QUILT:
measurements include 1/4" seams

CRIB:

background:	(4) 16" square
	(4) 3 1/2" x 41 1/2"
pink:	(16) J
	(4) K
	(1) 1 3/8" x width of fabric**
	(6) 1 1/2" x 15 1/2"
	(3) 1 1/2" x 33 1/2"
	(4) 1 1/2" x 41 1/2"
	binding: (1) 20" square
red:	(16) K
	(4) Q
	(16) loops
	(1) 1 3/4" x width of fabric**
green:	(64) A
	(64) B
	(4) J
	(4) N
	(16) Stems*: 3/4" x 6 1/2"
	(16) Stems*: 3/4" x 5"
gold:	(16) Q
	(1) 1" x width of fabric**
striped:**	(16) G

SINGLE:

background:	(4) 26" square
	(4) 6 1/2" x 72 1/2"
pink:	(16) K
	(4) L
	(1) 1 5/8" x width of fabric**
	(6) 2 1/2" x 25 1/2"
	(3) 2 1/2" x 56 1/2"
	(4) 2 1/2" x 72 1/2"
	binding: (1) 25" square
red:	(16) L
	(4) R
	(16) loops
	(1) 2" x width of fabric**
green:	(64) C
	(64) D
	(4) K
	(4) O
	(16) Stems*: 1" x 10"
	(16) Stems*: 1" x 8"
gold:	(16) R
	(1) 1 1/8" x width of fabric**
striped:**	(16) H

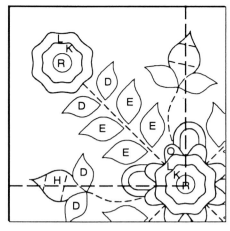

Whig Rose Queen block section

NOTE: *You will notice that templates G, H, and I call for striped fabric. These templates are the buds. Because of the smallness of some of the pieces, I felt it would be easier to construct a striped fabric, and cut the buds as one piece, rather than 3 small pieces.*

To construct the striped fabric, join the following strips, each 44" to 45" long, of gold, pink, and red fabric in the following groupings:

	CRIB	SINGLE	QUEEN	KING
gold	1"	1 1/8"	1 1/8"	1 1/4"
pink	1 3/8"	1 5/8"	1 5/8"	1 7/8"
red	1 3/4"	2"	2"	2 1/8"

Join the 3 strips using 1/4" seams to form a gold-pink-red striped band.

Press the band, so no pleats form along the seams.

Cut the proper template, using the dotted lines on the patterns G-H-I as seam-placement guidelines.

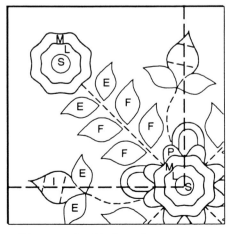

Whig Rose King block section

QUEEN:

background:	(4) 29" square
	(4) 8 1/2" x 84 1/2"
pink:	(16) K
	(4) L
	(1) 1 - 5/8" x width of fabric**
	(6) 3" x 28 - 1/2"
	(3) 3" x 64"
	(4) 3" x 84 - 1/2"
	binding: (1) 27" square
red:	(16) L
	(4) R
	(16) loops
	(1) 2" x width of fabric**
green:	(64) D
	(64) E
	(4) K
	(4) O
	(16) Stems*: 1" x 12"
	(16) Stems*: 1" x 8"
gold:	(16) R
	(1) 1 - 1/8" x width of fabric**
striped:**	(16) H

KING:

background:	(4) 34" square
	(4) 8 - 1/2" x 97 - 1/2"
pink:	(16) L
	(4) M
	(1) 1 - 7/8" x width of fabric**
	(6) 3 - 1/2" x 33 - 1/2"
	(3) 3 - 1/2" x 75 - 1/2"
	(4) 3 - 1/2" x 97 - 1/2"
	binding: (1) 29" square
red:	(16) M
	(4) S
	(16) loops
	(1) 2 - 1/8" x width of fabric**
green:	(64) E
	(64) F
	(4) L
	(4) P
	(16) Stems*: 1" x 13"
	(16) Stems*: 1" x 10"
gold:	(16) S
	(1) 1 - 1/4" x width of fabric**
striped:**	(16) I

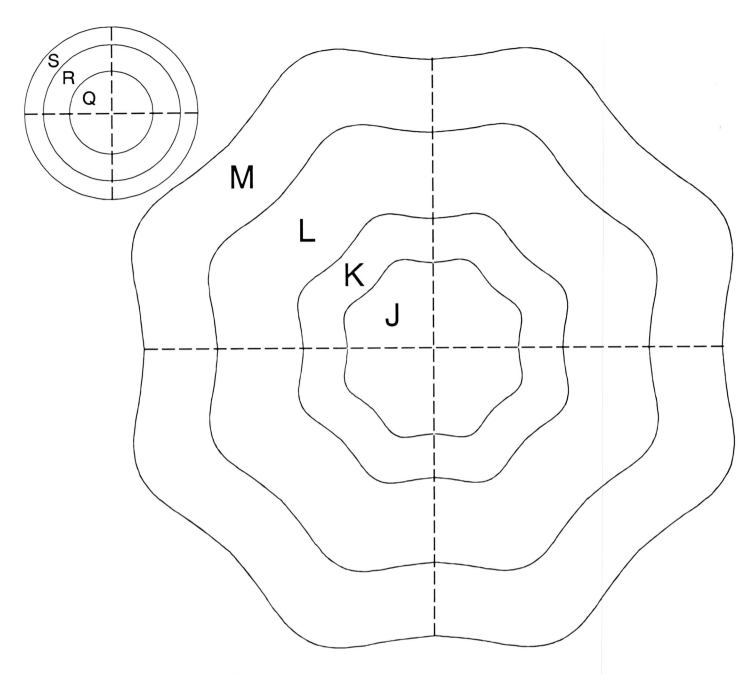

FREEZER PAPER APPLIQUÉ:

For the appliqué portion of this quilt, you may want to try this method using plastic coated freezer paper. I find it saves a lot of time in cutting, and gives designs that are more nicely shaped along the edges.

Cut each shape the required number of times out of freezer paper the exact size shown on the pattern pages. DO NOT add seam allowances. (To save time so you can get to the fun of stitching faster, trace one quarter the number needed of each template on freezer paper by laying the paper over the book and tracing through. Cut off your length of freezer paper 4 times the length covered by your tracings. Fold the paper

in quarters. Pin through all layers of the paper in each template. Cut through all four layers at once. This will give you templates that are mirror images of each other. That's Okay, as you will need that for the block. Leave them pinned together until you need them so they won't get jumbled and lost.)

Position the paper templates on the WRONG side of the fabric, WAXY side down, allowing a 1/4" seam allowance around each piece.

Using a DRY iron on a COTTON setting, fuse the paper to the fabric. If it isn't sticking well, increase the heat slightly. If repeated handling loosens the bond before you're ready to appliqué, just repress.

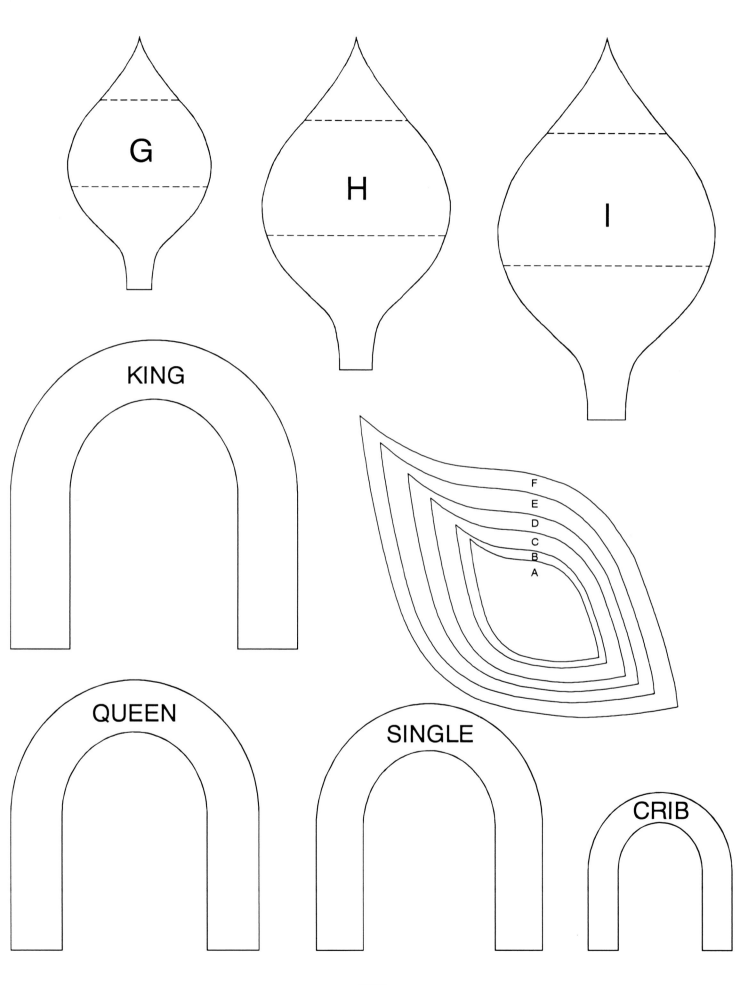

G

H

I

KING

QUEEN

SINGLE

CRIB

F
E
D
C
B
A

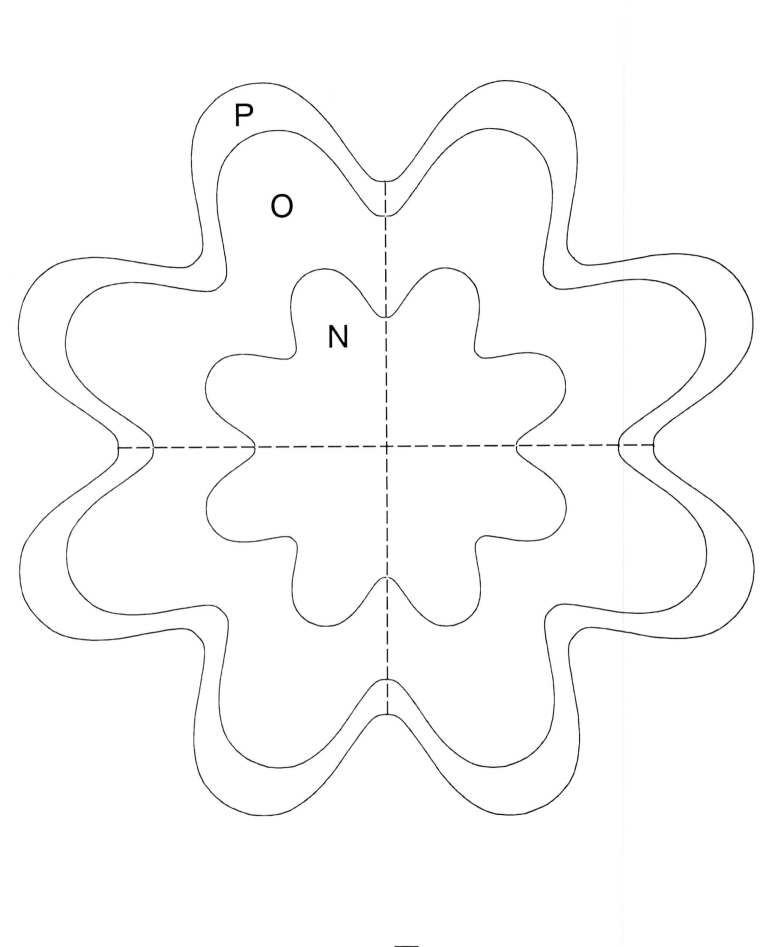

P

O

N

How to Make Narrow Even Stems:

Lay a piece of masking tape (3/4" wide for crib, 1" wide for single-queen-king) on the bias of the green fabric.

Cut the fabric along the edges of the tape to give you a strip the same width as the tape.
> HINT - cut fabric slightly longer than the tape, thereby giving you a handle to grab onto when you remove the tape.)

Stems will be cut from this length of fabric. Carefully remove the tape and set it aside. It can be used 3 or 4 more times before being discarded.

The cutting lengths listed are 1/2" longer than the finished stem length on the base block (to allow for seams at the ends of the stem). Fold fabric in half, wrong sides together. Finger press.

Mark placement guidelines on base block lightly with #3 pencil. Pin folded strip to the base block, positioning the raw edges along the line.

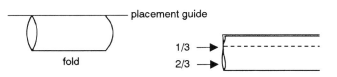

Using matching thread, stitch the strip to the base block, 1/3 of the way in from the raw edge. Use a backstitch for extra strength and smoother results.

Press the folded portion of the stem over the seam allowance, thereby covering it, and forming a narrow stem. Appliqué the folded edge to the base block. Press.

APPLIQUÉ OF THE WHIG ROSE QUILT:

Note that the base blocks (background fabric) have been cut slightly larger than need be. This is to give you a margin for error in an area that sometimes troubles stitchers. At times, the base block in appliqué "shrinks up" underneath the motifs stitched on it, causing the block to be too small when completed. By cutting the base block slightly larger than needed, you have a margin of error built in should this happen to you.

To prevent this from happening, be sure to pin motifs in place with small bites (A "bite" is how much fabric is "stitched" onto your pin. Large bites with your pins allows fabric layers to shift, causing inaccuracies). Also be sure to press the base block from the wrong side after the addition of each motif.

1. Mark stem placement guidelines on the base block. Stems are stitched in place first. Follow the procedures for *How to Make Narrow Even Stems*.

(Note: the initial stitching of the strips to the base blocks may be done by machine if desired. Take care not to stretch the strip when attaching it to the block.)

2. Loops may now be stitched in place, using freezer paper appliqué. One of the beauties of this method is that you can get smooth edges on your shapes. First, pin the motif to the base block with 3 or 4 pins to prevent it from shifting. Remember to take small bites with your pins.

HINT: Try pinning from the WRONG side of the base block. That way there will be no 'pin ends' for the thread to get tangled in.

3. With matching thread (single strand, 15" - 18" long), blindstitch shape in place, turning under the seam allowance as you go until it hugs the edge of the freezer paper. Clip seam allowance if necessary, but to not cut into freezer paper. The freezer paper will give you a firm edge to work against. Do not stitch through the paper. Do not bend the edge of the paper when you fold under the seam allowance. Press from the wrong side when stitching is complete.

The freezer paper may be removed in one of two ways:

1. When stitching is complete, turn the block to the wrong side, make a slit in the base fabric only, along the grain, and carefully remove the freezer paper. It pulls away easily. If desired, you may want to whip-stitch the slit closed.

Notes: when making slits, always cut along the grain, leaving a 1/4" space between the slit and the stitching.

If whip-stitching the slit closed, take care to merely draw the edges so they touch. DO NOT overlap. Overlapping would cause the block to shrink up and ripple.

~OR~

2. When you have blindstitched all but about 1" of the shape, finger press the fold of the remaining seam allowance, then gently remove the freezer paper. Complete the blindstitching.

HINT: For best results, press frequently as you applique. Use a dry iron (steam causes stretching and distortion). Press from the WRONG side of the piece, placing the piece on a padded ironing board so as to avoid causing shiny spots.

For ease in handling, you may construct the blossom units, then stitch the completed blossom unit in place on the base block. To do so:

1. Fold the components of each blossom in quarters to find the centers. Lay the center circle on its layer of the blossom, matching the creases and center, and stitch the circle in place.

NOTE: Stitch the circle to the FABRIC ONLY of the blossom, not through the freezer paper.

2. Position the circle-blossom unit on the next layer of the blossom, again matching creases and centers, and stitch in place.

3. Repeat until the blossom unit is complete. Press. Position on the base block. Appliqué in place. Remove freezer paper of all layers after the unit has been attached to the base block.

4. To remove papers, follow directions at left, doing one layer at a time. (Slit through the base block to remove the paper from the largest layer of the blossom. Slit through the largest layer of the blossom to remove the paper from the next layer of the blossom, etc. Having paper layers in there protects you from cutting an area you don't wish to cut. Whipstitching, if desired, only needs to be done on the base block after all papers have been removed.

5. The four striped buds may be appliquéd in place.

6. Leaves may be appliquéd. Note that leaves on opposite sides of each stem are mirror images of each other.

7. Press block. NOTE: If you chose NOT to whip stitch the slits closed, take care that the iron does not get caught in the slit and tear the block.

8. Construct 4 blocks. Trim to the proper size, removing any excess margin for error.
   crib: 15 1/2" (includes seams)
   single: 25 1/2" (includes seams)
   queen: 28 1/2" (includes seams)
   king: 33 1/2" (includes seams)

You are now ready to join the blocks with pink sashing.

1. Using the 6 sashing strips of length equal to the blocks, make 2 rows in the following sequence:
    strip + block + strip + block + strip
    Press.

2. Using the 3 sashing strip of equal length, next assemble the rows.
    strip + row + strip + row + strip
    Press.

3. Join one remaining sashing strip to each border strip. These 4 sashed borders may now be added to the quilt top, mitering in the corners.

To Attach Borders to the Quilt Top:
Refer to *Finishing Finesse*

It deals with proper technique for attaching borders, how to avoid rippling edges, how to miter corners, and how to bind the edges.

The Appliqué of Nature...
Star and Tulip Quilt
COLOR PHOTO PAGE 61

Little is known about this quilt, other than that it is one of those rare treasures that was purchased by the owner for $5 at a time when quilts had not yet captivated the collecting market. Its combination of an eight point star with a single tulip blossom makes it a charming one-of-a-kind design.

The tulip has long been a favorite choice for appliqué. In Persia, it is said that upon hearing of the death of his beloved Shirin, young Farhad flung himself off a rocky cliff to his death. From his blood sprang the tulip, forever making it the symbol of perfect love. Thus it is thought that the Rose of Sharon, as told in the Bible's Song of Solomon, was actually a tulip. Its name, taken in part from the Persian and Turkish word for "turban", reflects its Oriental roots. First cultivated as a garden flower in Turkey, probably around 1500, the tulip was introduced to Europeans when Emperor Ferdinand I's ambassador from the Holy Roman Empire was sent to the Sultan of Turkey in 1543. Taking seeds and possibly also bulbs back to Vienna, the Ambassador thus introduced tulips to Europe.

In 1593, botanist Charles de l'Ecluse moved from Vienna to accept an appointment as Professor of Botany in the Netherlands. Planning to gain his fortune by introducing tulips to the Netherlands, he took bulbs with him to his new home. But alas, when the price he asked was too high, his home was broken into, the bulbs were stolen, and the Netherlands began the industry for which they have gained worldwide fame. Charles died poor, while tulips captured the imagination of the countryside. They became the object of gambling and speculation, so much so that in the 1630's, fortunes were won or lost over the sale of tulip bulbs. Between 1634 and 1637, one of the scarlet and white striped "sember augustus", of which only twelve bulbs were said to be in existence, was sold for 5,500 florins[1], or the 1991 equivalent of $10,991.20.

By 1730, there were said to be over 1300 varieties of tulips available. Unlike most flowers, the tulip seems not to have had medicinal purposes. It was grown purely for the pleasure it brought.

"When a young man presents a tulip to his mistress...he gives her to understand, by the general colour of the flower, that he is on fire with her beauty, and by the black base of it, that his heart is burnt to a coal."

Sir John Chardin, Travels into Persia, 1686[2]

Introduced to England in 1578, the tulip soon spread to other countries on the continent. A favorite blossom of the Netherlands, the tulip came to the New World with Dutch settlers. It is second only to the rose as a favorite choice for appliqué renditions in quiltmaking.

It is not known when or who made this charming quilt, but its maker leaves behind a tantalizing trail of questions to ponder. On first glance, this is a standard block quilt, set with plain sashing strips. Small pieced eight point stars form the center for a larger star, with tulip blossoms appliquéd between the points. That is where we must stop. On closer examination, the only truth is that the tulips have been appliquéd.

In fact, the quilt top is actually one piece of cloth upon which the stars have been positioned, then appliquéd in place. The technique of creating appliquéd triangles is one that began appearing in the early 1800's, first as a decoration on clothing in imitation of more expensive lace trims, and seldom seen on quilts past the 1860's. Referred to as Van Dyck points or dogtoothing, this form of decoration was inspired by Anton Van Dyck, portrait painter of the early 1600's, renowned for his extraordinary ability to paint rich fabrics and ornamentations with astounding realism.

Seen years later as a way to embellish clothing without the expense of lace, fabric was manipulated by folding to form the triangular point edging so often portrayed in Van Dyck's paintings. Applied in appliqué fashion along the interior of the garment's edge, this form of decoration was sometimes formed by folding bits of cloth that were then attached along the exterior of the garment's edge, much as "prairie points" are executed today.

Recently reintroduced to American quiltmakers by such well known quilt experts as Elly Sienkiewicz, sawtooth edging now graces the edges of many of today's Baltimore-style album quilts. Its use on this quilt of unknown vintage is a curiosity to be sure. Made much more recently than the 1800-1860 time period when this technique first appeared on quilts, this quilt predates the current trend of sawtoothing on quilts by at least 50 years. Where, then, did the quilter become familiar with this unusual technique? Was it a purchased pattern? Did she see an antique quilt with appliquéd points that inspired her to construct a star in appliqué rather than piecing? Why did she choose to appliqué the quilt as a whole cloth quilt rather than in blocks? Quilted lines create the illusion of seamlines and sashes, while their actual use certainly would have been a much more manageable way to construct the quilt. Why, if the quilt top is one large piece of cloth, is the back pieced?

In examining the tulip, we discover that it is executed in four separate pieces. A logical template configuration if elements of the tulip are multicolored, why was this method of construction chosen for a monochromatic representation of the tulip? While we may never know the answers to these questions, it is intriguing to wonder what may have been going through the quilter's mind as she worked on this unusual quilt.

Quiltmakers of today may construct the quilt in easier to manage blocks, with sashing set between. Given in three sizes, these directions provide you with a multitude of design possibilities. Whether set with sashes, alternate blocks, or on point, the Star and Tulip quilt is one you are sure to enjoy.

The zest of hand-dyed and marbleized fabrics gives a wonderful freshness to this charming pattern. Fabrics courtesy of Sheryll Robbins, New York Beauty Dye Works.

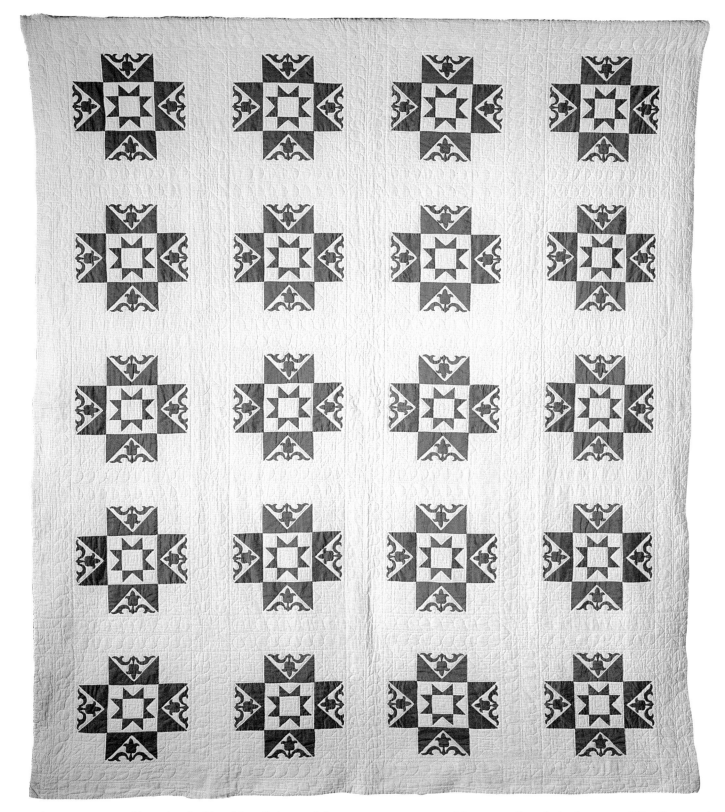

74 1/2" x 92" Executed in teal and white, this quilt is one of those rare treasures rescued from an antique dealer for a mere $5 by its current owner, Jeannette Keyser.

STAR AND TULIP QUILT
finished block - 13" square

SINGLE: 74 1/2" X 92"
20 blocks - 4 x 5 block layout

YARDAGES:

background: 6 yds.
star/tulip: 2 3/4 yds.
binding: 7/8 yds.
backing: 5 1/4 yds.

FULL*: 92" X 92"
25 blocks - 5 x 5 block layout

YARDAGES:

background: 7 1/2 yds.
star/tulip: 3 1/2 yds.
binding: 7/8 yds.
backing: 7 yds.

* no pillow tuck in on this size

FULL/QUEEN: 92" X 109 1/2"
30 blocks - 5 x 6 block layout

YARDAGES:

background: 8 1/4 yds.
star/tulip: 4 yds.
binding: 1 yds.
backing: 8 yds.

---

measurements include 1/4" seams

	SINGLE		FULL		FULL/QUEEN	
	Size	#Pieces	Size	#Pieces	Size	#Pieces
BACKGROUND FABRIC						
blocks	13 1/2" square	20	13 1/2"square	25	13 1/2"square	30
short sash	5" x 13 1/2"	24	5" x 13 1/2"	30	5" x 13 1/2"	35
long sash	5" x 92 1/2"	5	5" x 92 1/2"	6	5" x 109 1/2"	6
STAR/TULIP FABRIC						
small stars	1 7/8" x 2 3/4"	80	1 7/8" x 2 3/4"	100	1 7/8" x 2 3/4"	120
large stars	3 3/4" x 6"	80	3 3/4" x 6"	100	3 3/4" x 6"	120
tulip stem		80		100		120
tulip blossom		80		100		120
leaf		80		100		120
reverse leaf		80		100		120
BINDING						
binding	27" square	1	29" square	1	31" square	1
from this cut...	340" binding 2" wide**		380" binding 2" wide**		420" binding 2" wide**	

**see *Finishing Finesse* for directions on cutting binding

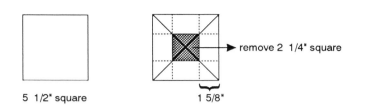

5 1/2" square   1 5/8"

remove 2 1/4" square

GENERAL DIRECTIONS:

Finished Size: 13" square
Blocks: cut size: 13 1/2" square

1. Cut template 5 1/2" square.

2. Draw diagonal lines corner to corner as shown.

3. Remove a 2 1/4" square from the center of the template by drawing lines 1 5/8" in from each side of the square. This results in a 2 1/4" square in the center of the template. Removing this square gives you a window template.

4. Cut base block 13 1/2" square.

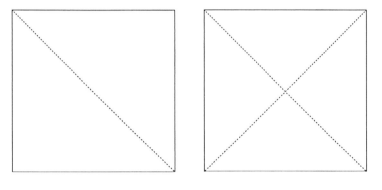

5. Fold base block in half on the diagonal, corner to corner. Finger press. Repeat, folding along the other diagonal. This divides the block into quarters.

   HINT: Do not crease with an iron, otherwise the creases will be too difficult to remove.

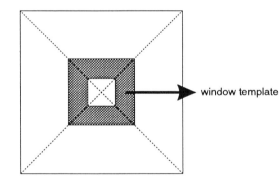

window template

6. Center the window template on the right side of the base block by aligning the corners of the window template with the diagonal creases of the base block.

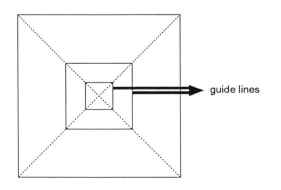

guide lines

7. Trace edge of inner window and outer edge of template to give you placement guides for construction of stars.

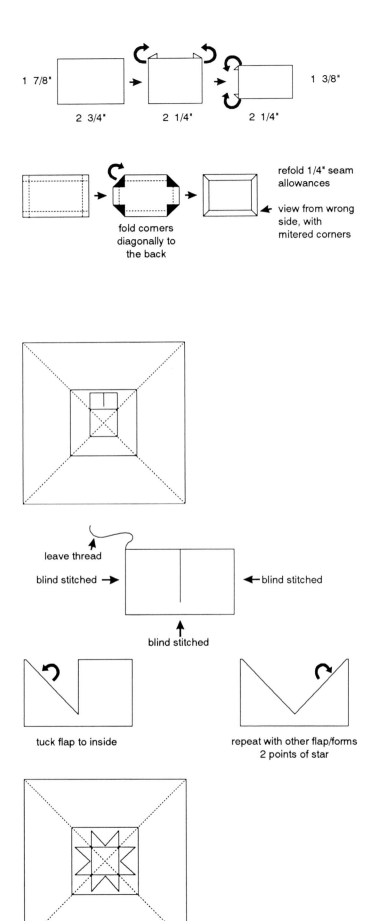

INNER STAR:

1. Cut 4 pieces 1 7/8" x 2 3/4".

2. Press under 1/4" on all edges. Pieces now measure 1 3/8" x 2 1/4".

To reduce bulk, miter seams at corners. Open the seams. Fold seam allowance at corner on diagonal as shown, across corner, to wrong side. Refold seams along original creases.

3. Fold in half to find the center of the length.

4. Make a 1 1/8" long cut along the crease (1/4" will remain uncut).

5. Position the long uncut edge of one rectangle along one side of the 2 1/4" inner square as shown.

6. Appliqué down one side, across the bottom (keeping the edge of the rectangle in alignment with the guideline on the base block), and up the other side. DO NOT CLIP YOUR THREAD.

7. Tuck the flaps formed by the slash to the inside. Because the sides are stitched in place, you will have a "wall to abut against" as you fold the flap to the inside. Press.

8. Appliqué the V-shape just formed by the flap-folds. This completes two points of the star. Press.

9. Repeat with the remaining units on the remaining three sides of the inner star.

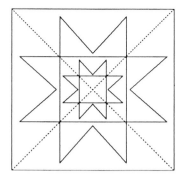

OUTER STAR

1. Cut four pieces 3 3/4 " x 6".

2. Repeat the above procedure, positioning the units along the outer placement guide traced onto the base block. The slash down the center of the unit will be 3" long. Press.

TULIP

1. Cut 4 blossoms, 4 stems, 4 leaves, and 4 leaves reversed for each block. To do so, trace around each template on the right side of the fabric. Cut a scant 1/4" larger than the tracing.

2. Clip seam allowances at inner curves and inner points (cleavage areas).

3. Follow this order of appliqué: leaves, stem, blossom.

NOTE: it is not necessary to turn under the area of the stem which will be covered by the blossom.

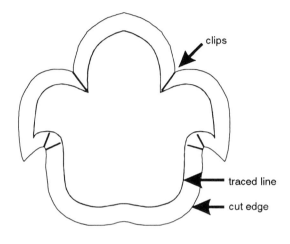

clips

traced line

cut edge

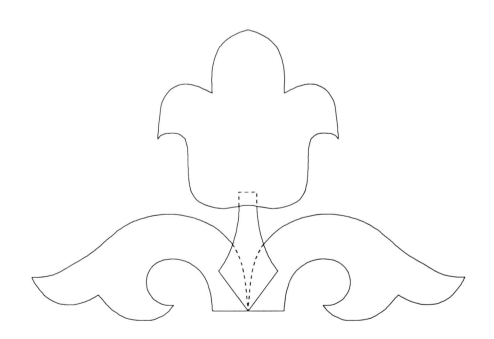

Hand Appliqué How -To's

Templates cut out of sturdy template material may be used over and over again without becoming distorted along the edge by repeated tracings. Many quilt shops sell light-weight plastic expressly for this purpose.

To prevent your fabric from slipping as you trace, place a sheet of medium grain sand paper grit side up on your work surface. Lay fabric on top, right side up. Position templates on top, allowing 1/4" excess around all edges for seam allowance. Trace around edge of template with a #3 pencil.

The pencil line you have just traced is the line along which you will fold under the seam allowance. It is also the stitching line. Cut fabric 1/4" larger than the pencil line.

Clip the seam allowance only along inner curves and inner points (cleavage areas). Clip to within two or three threads of the seamline.

For the most invisible stitching, use thread that matches the color of the shape being stitched. Regular sewing thread will result in more invisible stitches than quilting thread. Fine needles will also result in more invisible stitches. Size 10 or 11 quilting needles are recommended.

To more easily manage appliqué, begin stitching along a fairly straight area of the motif so it may be anchored to the base block before having to deal with any tricky areas such as points or curves.

Finger press the seam allowance under as you get to it, turning on the pencil marking as you go.

Using a strand of thread 15" - 18" long (finger tip to elbow length), knot the end. Begin by bringing the needle from the underside of the appliqué motif to the top side of the motif, on the pencil line. As you then tuck in the seam allowance, you will encase the knot and hide it.

The thread is now coming out of the fold of the motif, on the pencil line. The ladder stitch gives very invisible stitches. It is done in two steps. You are in position to do step one.

Pencil leads have different degrees of hardness. The higher the number, the harder the lead. Harder lead means the pencil point will not dull as quickly, resulting in a thinner, more accurate line, and it won't smudge as readily, resulting in cleaner, neater work.

We usually work with number 2 pencils (if your pencil doesn't have a number on it, or has advertising on it instead, it probably is a number 2). Number 3 leads are slightly harder and will give better results.

Mechanical pencils that use number 3 leads are available in office and school supply outlets, and do not require constant resharpening.

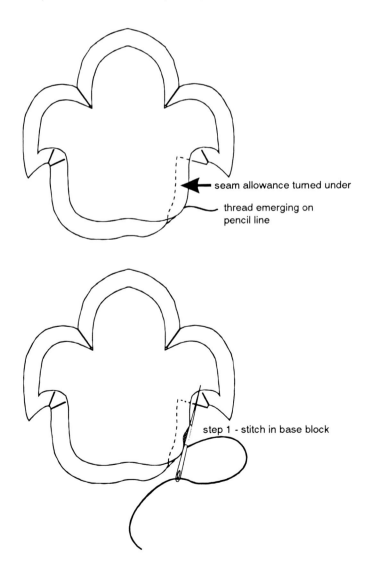

seam allowance turned under

thread emerging on pencil line

step 1 - stitch in base block

1.   With the thread emerging from the fold, insert the tip of the needle in the base block, even

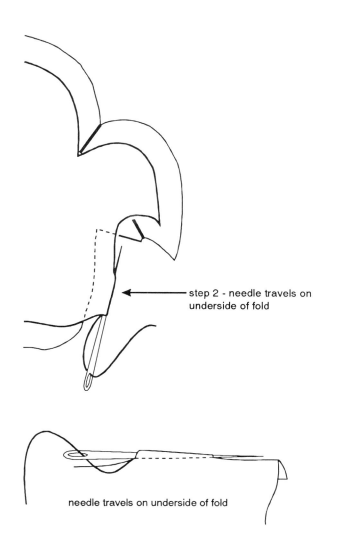

step 2 - needle travels on underside of fold

needle travels on underside of fold

HINT- If you wear bifocals or trifocals:

When you stitch in the base block, instead of positioning your needle so it appears to you to be NEXT TO THE FOLD, position the needle so it appears to you to be just under the edge of the fold of the appliqué motif. This will correct for the distortion you get from your eyeglasses.

with where the thread is coming out of the other layer of fabric, and right next to the fold. DO NOT PULL THROUGH. Take a small stitch (1/16" - 1/8" long) in the BASE BLOCK ONLY. Pull the needle through to complete the stitch.

This completes step one. You are now in position to do step two.

2.   Insert the tip of the needle in the fold of the appliqué (on the pencil line), even with where the thread is coming out of the other layer of fabric. DO NOT PULL THROUGH. Take a small stitch (1/16" - 1/8"), allowing the needle to travel on the underside of the fold, and emerge on the pencil line of the fold. Pull through.

This completes step two. You are now in position to repeat step one.

Note that you are never stitching through more than one layer of cloth at a time. This makes the stitching much easier to accomplish, and gives a stitch that hides itself as you go along.

This is called the ladder stitch.

What makes this stitch invisible is always inserting the needle in the new layer even with where the thread is emerging from the old layer. If you advance the needle forward, the result will be an angled stitch which will show along the edge of the motif.

Tension - Pull your stitches tight enough so the motif hugs itself to the base block without becoming gathered along the edges. If you can either see under the motif along the edges, or if on the wrong side of the base block the stitches appear to bubble up, you are not pulling your stitches tightly enough.

As you approach "tricky areas", stop stitching 1/2" from the area in question. This gives you room to adjust your sewing technique to properly handle the tricky areas.

Cleavage areas - Due to the clipped seam allowance, there will be no fold to ladder stitch in for about 1/8" on each side of the clip. In this area, it is necessary to do an overcast stitch to bind off the raw edge of the motif that results at the clip.

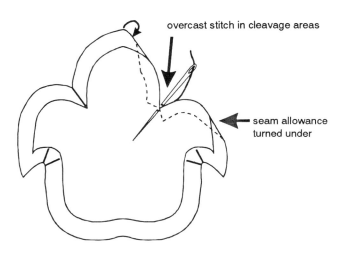

overcast stitch in cleavage areas

seam allowance turned under

point as viewed from the wrong side

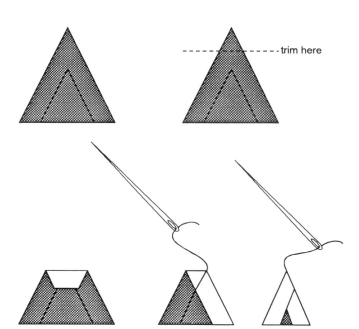

trim here

To do so, when the thread is emerging from the fold of the appliqué motif, insert the tip of the needle in the base block, but when you scoop the tip of the needle up to make the stitch, come up through two layers of fabric, stitching through the base block and the edge of the appliqué.

To make the next stitch, allow the thread to go over the fold of the appliqué, insert the tip of the needle in the base block BEHIND THE MOTIF, AND SLIGHTLY BELOW THE POSITION OF THE FOLD (you will not be able to see where the point is piercing the base block), and scoop the needle up through the two layers of fabric as before.

As you pull the needle to complete the stitch, the thread will curl the edge of the motif under, thereby encasing the raw edge at the clip and burying the stitch so it is barely visible.

Repeat the "tuck behind and below" procedure for three to five stitches, until you are past the clip into "seam allowance territory" again. Resume the ladder stitch.

Points - Stop stitching 1/2" before the point. To reduce bulk, trim off any seam allowance in excess of 1/4" beyond the point.

Make your first fold across the point, so the penciled point comes right to the fold.

Turn under the seam allowance along the edge you were just stitching along. Resume stitching, adjusting your stitches as necessary so the last stitch will result in thread emerging from the point of the motif.

Finger press.

Turn under the remaining seam allowance, keeping a hold of the thread as you do so. Keeping tension on the thread emerging from the point as you fold will give you extra control in keeping the point crisp. Make your first stitch near the point a tiny one, so as to anchor the crispness in. Proceed with the ladder stitch.

When the appliqué is complete, press from the wrong side to avoid causing shiny spots on your block.

Star and Tulip Quilt, single (74 1/2" x 92"), 20 blocks, 4 x 5 block layout

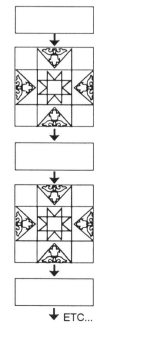

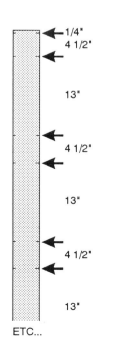

1/4"
4 1/2"

13"

4 1/2"

13"

4 1/2"

13"

ETC...

ETC...

CONSTRUCTION:

1. Follow General Directions for construction of the required number of quilt blocks.

2. Using the quilt diagram as a guide, join quilt blocks to short sashing strips to create rows. Press.

3. On the wrong side of each long sashing strip, within the seam allowance area, make the following guide marks:

   Measure from the raw edge, down the length.
   a. Place the first marking 1/4" from end.

   b. Make a second mark 4 1/2" from the first. (The seamlines of a short sashing strip will match to these marks).

   c. The next mark is 13" away. (The seamline of a block will match this mark).

   d. Repeat markings, alternating a 4 1/2" spacing with a 13" spacing, ending with a 4 1/2" spacing, followed by a 1/4" space for the outer seam allowance.

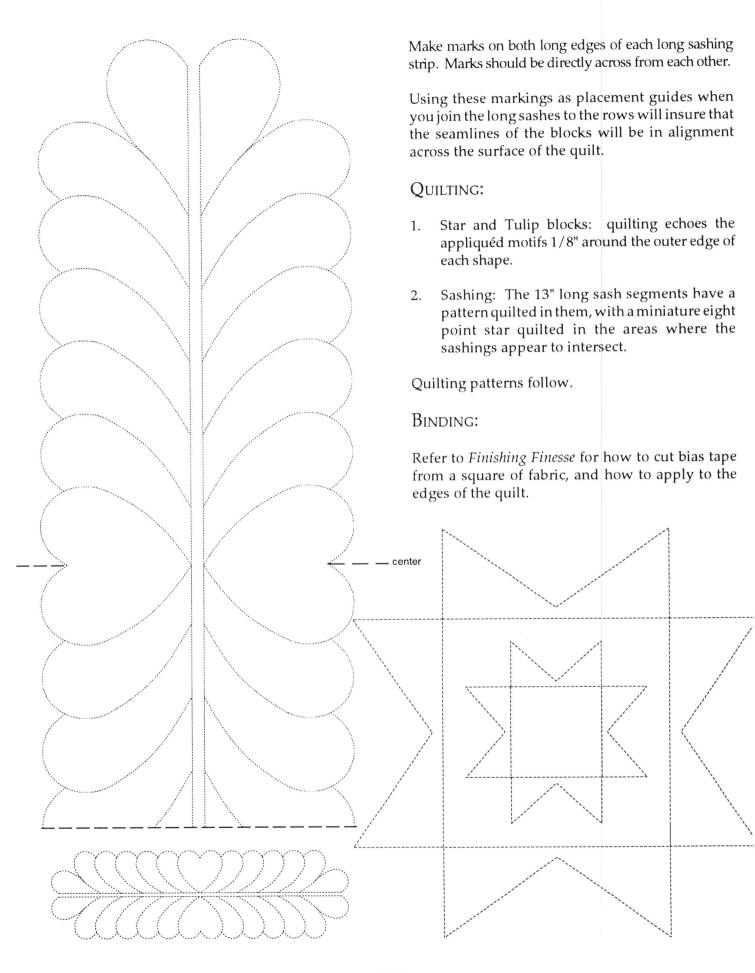

Make marks on both long edges of each long sashing strip. Marks should be directly across from each other.

Using these markings as placement guides when you join the long sashes to the rows will insure that the seamlines of the blocks will be in alignment across the surface of the quilt.

QUILTING:

1. Star and Tulip blocks: quilting echoes the appliquéd motifs 1/8" around the outer edge of each shape.

2. Sashing: The 13" long sash segments have a pattern quilted in them, with a miniature eight point star quilted in the areas where the sashings appear to intersect.

Quilting patterns follow.

BINDING:

Refer to *Finishing Finesse* for how to cut bias tape from a square of fabric, and how to apply to the edges of the quilt.

center

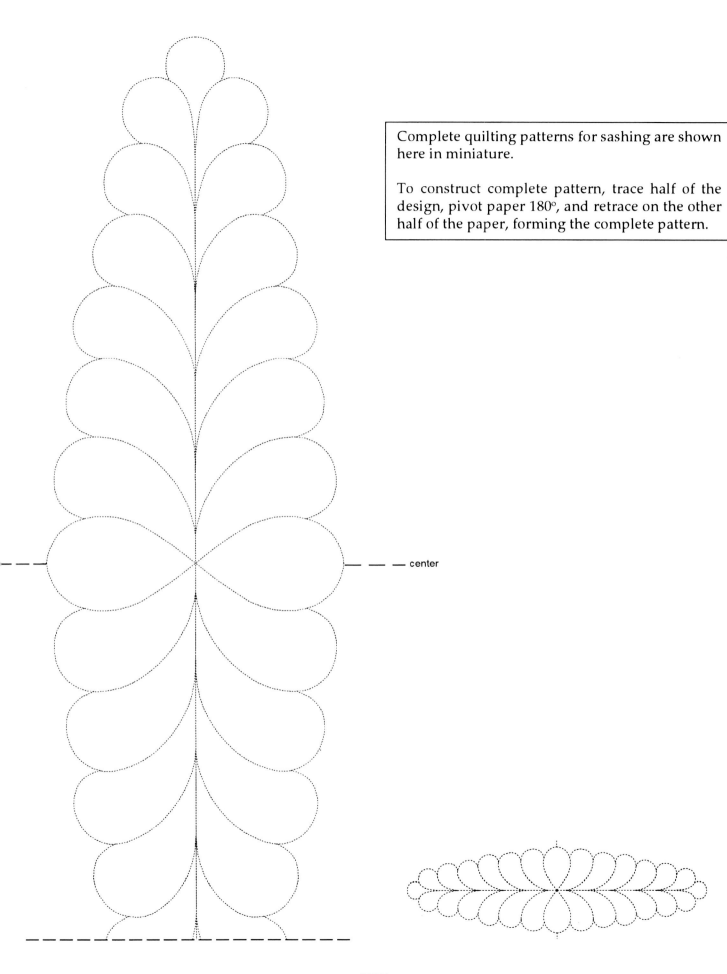

Complete quilting patterns for sashing are shown here in miniature.

To construct complete pattern, trace half of the design, pivot paper 180°, and retrace on the other half of the paper, forming the complete pattern.

center

Young Man's Fancy...
or Goose in the Pond

COLOR PHOTO PAGE **74**

Red and white is a color combination which has been finding favor with quilters since the 1840's when a truly colorfast red became available for the first time. Dubbed Turkey Red as a reflection of its eastern Mediterranean origin, it was a red that remained fast, a skill that was not learned by European dyers until the mid 1700's. It was a complicated process using the madder root that required anywhere from thirteen to twenty steps to achieve. Because of its long and complicated procedure, turkey red was not made in American mills until after 1868, when alizarin, the coloring agent in madder, became available synthetically, thereby simplifying the dying procedure. As the popular fabric became more readily available, more and more quilts were made using reds. Sometimes solid, sometimes printed over, red was used in red and white quilts as a popular color scheme for nearly one hundred years.[1]

The simplicity of the elements of this pattern make it as appealing today as it was in the early 1800's. Ruth Finley, in *Old Patchwork Quilts* (1929), documented this pattern as having been found on a quilt made before 1810. "A more elaborate nine-patch, probably of Massachusetts origin, was called *A Young Man's Fancy*. This quilt is constantly bobbing up in all parts of the country and, what is rather extraordinary, under the same name."[2]

Mrs. Finley may not have been acquainted with Ladies' Art Company, credited as the first mail-order quilt pattern company, for they referred to the same pattern as *Goose in the Pond* in 1898. And that is the name given to it by Ruby McKim in her 1931 classic *101 Patchwork Patterns*, where it was referred to as "one of those homey old-fashioned names which grace so many patchworks."[3]

The discerning quilter of today would probably categorize this as a five patch pattern, that is , one which can be drawn on a grid of five equal divisions horizontally and vertically. The shape of the design elements, while giving it that "old-fashioned homey" quality, is one which adapts well to some of the speed techniques so much in favor with

Goose in the Pond
Pattern #202
13"
Price List of Finished Blocks:
$.50 each $5.50 per dozen
"The blocks are made only in the size given below the illustration of this design. We make the design in any combination of colors desired, using the best muslin and colored materials."

Ladies' Art Catalog, 1928

quilters of the 1990's. Use of a rotary cutter would allow for quick and easy construction of large blocks, which are then complemented by the quilted sampler that appears in the alternate plain blocks in this lovely quilt.

Much attention has been paid to sampler quilts, both pieced and appliquéd, as one way in which a quilter could keep a catalog of sorts of favorite patterns. But virtually no attention has been paid to quilting samplers. Not nearly as common as pieced or appliquéd samplers, quilting samplers are the almost hidden treasures of some quilts with alternate plain squares, each of which contains a different quilting design.

The set style chosen by the stitcher was a matter of personal preference, sometimes governed by the amount of fabric on hand, or the number of blocks one had stitched, or even the desired size of the finished quilt. But another consideration that may have been overlooked is the opportunity for the making of a quilting sampler. Setting blocks together with alternate plain squares allowed stitchers not only the construction option to create fewer pieced or appliquéd blocks, but also the design consideration to frame each block, in effect, by having more background in evidence.

But to the quilter, it gave her the venue to record favorite quilting patterns, changing design from block to block, subtly changing the textural relief that surrounded the more obvious colored designs of her quilt. Quilts such as these are a treasure for lovers of quilting patterns. Less frequently recorded than any other patterns available to quilters, quilting patterns found in samplers such as these provide a bonanza of patterns to the quilter. While quilted samplers appear to have been in fashion in the early 1800's, it is a style that was rarely seen after the Civil War.

This is in itself rather ironic. In 1846, the lives of quilters were made easier by the "invention" of sheet batting. Prior to this time, wadding, or loose cotton, was laid out on a stretched backing until it formed a smooth layer of uniform thickness. To prepare a cotton batt, women needed 12 pounds of raw cotton, of which two-thirds would be seed and one-third usable cotton for the batt, increasing our appreciation of antique quilts all the more.

Templates for quilting patterns took many shapes. Sometimes cookie-cutter type tools were stamped first in a cinnamon-cornstarch mixture that was then stamped onto the quilt, leaving a powdery outline of the pattern to be followed. Other enterprising quilters traced around templates with a boot spur, leaving a dotted track on the cloth for stitchers to follow, and giving rise to the tool we now know as the tracing wheel.

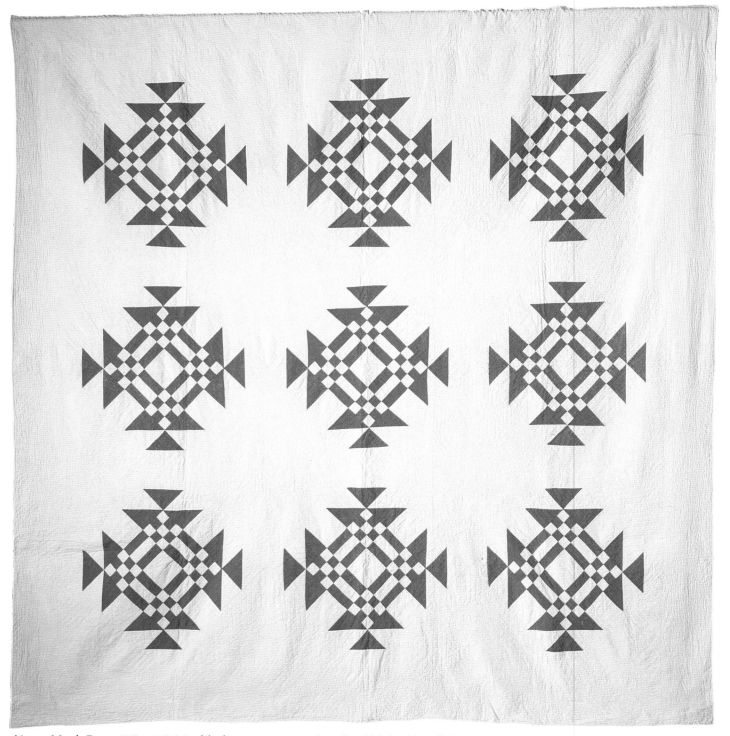

Young Man's Fancy 77" x 77" Set with alternate expanses of unpieced fabric, this quilt becomes the almost hidden treasure known as the "quilting sampler". This quilt is one of those rare beauties that was so treasured, it did not receive hard use. The pencil lines marking the quilting patterns are still visible to those who look closely. Collection of Gene and Jeanne Wilber.

101" x 101" Made by Elizabeth Ann Darst, Circleville, Ohio, 1840, at the age of 22, one year before her marriage. The Mariner's Compass blocks in this quilt complement the beauty and craftsmanship of the quilting and trapunto in the alternate blocks. Choosing a different design for each block, what was once plain becomes richly decorated in an unexpected tapestry of texture, giving us a quilting sampler extraordinaire. Collection of Elizabeth M. Holden, a great-granddaughter of the quiltmaker. First published in The Quilt Digest 4. Used by permission of The Quilt Digest Press.

Young Man's Fancy
Construction:
15" blocks

Template construction for "speed piecing" this block acquaints the quilter with four different machine construction techniques:

A: Squares: The template for a plain square in this technique requires an additional 1/4" drawn around all 4 sides of the finished square.

Example: for a 15" block, A finishes to 3".

The template, therefore, including the 1/4" seam allowance, is 3 1/2" square.

B: Half-square triangles: the 'magic number' that needs to be added to the finished square size for this "stitch-then-cut half-square triangle technique" is 7/8".

Example: for a 15" block, B finishes to 3". In the template for B, 3" + 7/8" = 3 7/8" square.

C: The striped unit: the strips divide this unit into equal thirds. In our example, each strip must finish to 1" wide in order to equal a 3" square when joined. Strips, including seam allowances, will be cut 1 1/2" wide.

D: The checked unit is made by sewing strips of fabric together to make a band, slicing the band to make rows of squares, then joining three rows of squares to form the checked pattern. Strips, including seam allowances, will be cut 1 1/2" wide.

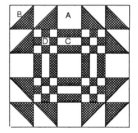

YARDAGE REQUIREMENTS

	CRIB	SINGLE
Finished Size	39" x 39"	77" x 77"
Block Size	7 1/2"	15"
# Blocks	9	9
YARDAGE:		
white	2 yds.	5 1/2 yds.
red	3/4 yd.	1 1/2 yds.
binding*	1/2 yd.	3/4 yd.
backing	1 1/4 yds.	4 1/2 yds.

binding = color of your choice

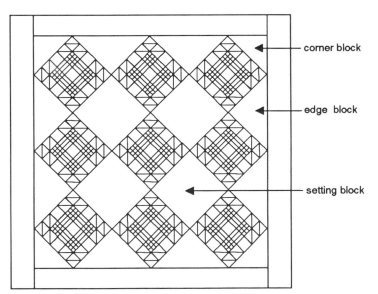

corner block

edge block

setting block

YOUNG MAN'S FANCY
MODELED AFTER THE RED AND WHITE QUILT SHOWN ON PAGE 74.

Directions are given for two sizes. Both sizes contain nine patchwork blocks, with the motifs in each size scaled to be proportionate to the size of the quilt. For ease in construction, go through the pattern, and mark the measurements that apply to the size you are making.

CUTTING FOR YOUNG MAN'S FANCY:
measurements include 1/4" seam allowance

CRIB:

white:	(4) corner blocks
	(8) edge blocks
	(4) 8" x 8" setting blocks
	borders: (2) 4" x 33"
	(2) 4" x 40"
	"A" (45)
	"B" Trace* (54)
	strips (7) 1" x width of fabric
red:	"B" Pin to white fabric used for B*
	strips (8) 1" x width of fabric
binding:	(1) 19" square

* see construction directions pg 79

SINGLE:

white:	(4) corner blocks
	(8) edge blocks
	(4) 15 1/2" x 15 1/2" setting blocks
	borders: (2) 7" x 65"
	(2) 7" x 78"
	"A" (45)
	"B" Trace* (54)
	strips (11) 1 1/2" x width of fabric
red:	"B" Pin to white fabric used for B*
	strips (13) 1 1/2" x width of fabric
binding:	(1) 26" square

* see construction directions pg 79

The simplicity of triangles and squares creates one of those "homey old-fashioned patterns" quilt lovers are continually drawn to. Known as both Young Man's Fancy and Goose in the Pond, we can only guess at the inspiration that suggested both names. Collection of The Strawberry Patch Calico Shop.

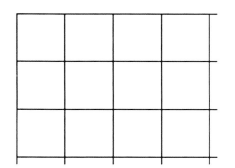

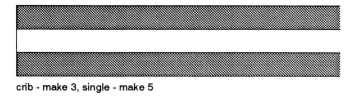

crib - make 3, single - make 5

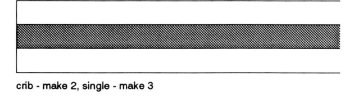

crib - make 2, single - make 3

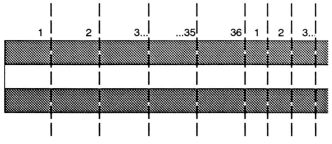

crib example (cut 36 2" slices then 36 1" slices)

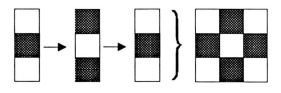

YOUNG MAN'S FANCY BLOCK

TO CONSTRUCT HALF SQUARE TRIANGLES ("B" IN FINISHED BLOCK)

This method uses the same technique used in the Bear's Paw quilt, allowing you to sew, then cut, resulting in two triangles that have already been pieced together.

1. Place red and white fabrics right sides together. On the wrong side of the white fabric, draw squares as shown:

crib quilt: squares are 2 3/8" square - draw 54

single quilt: squares are 3 7/8" square - draw 54

Follow steps 2 through 6 in the Bear's Paw construction of half square triangles, pages 36-37. You should have a total of 108 pieced squares when done.

STRIPED UNITS

1. Join strips to form bands as needed below:

crib - join 1" strips to form:
            3 bands of red/white/red
            2 bands of white/red/white

single - join 1 -1/2" strips to form:
            5 bands of red/white/red
            3 bands of white/red/white

Press. Be sure there are no pleats along seamlines.

2. Cut bands as follows:

crib: red/white/red   (36) 2" slices
                             (36) 1" slices
        white/red/white   (72) 1" slices

single: red/white/red   (36) 3 1/2" slices
                             (36) 1 1/2" slices
        white/red/white   (72) 1 1/2" slices

3. Wide slices are ready to use as piece "C" in construction of blocks. Set aside.

4. Narrow slices may be joined to form checkerboard units (D). Join as shown, matching seams. Press.

Construction of Block

Join units as shown. Press. Make 9 blocks.

Refer to the quilt diagram on page 77 for joining the pieced blocks to the setting units.

Border strips on this quilt are not mitered. The lengths you cut were a little longer than necessary to give you a margin for error.

See *Finishing Finesse* for directions on where to measure your quilt top to determine how long the shorter borders should be. Attach the shorter borders to the top and bottom of the quilt. Measure the resulting length of the quilt top to determine the correct length of the remaining two border strips. Join these to the sides of the quilt.

The quilt top is now complete. You are free to mark the white areas with the quilting patterns of your choice, sandwich the quilt top with the batting and backing, and begin quilting.

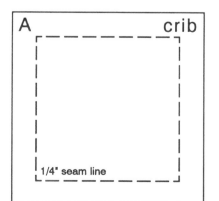

A   crib

1/4" seam line

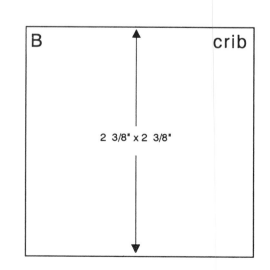

B   crib

2 3/8" x 2 3/8"

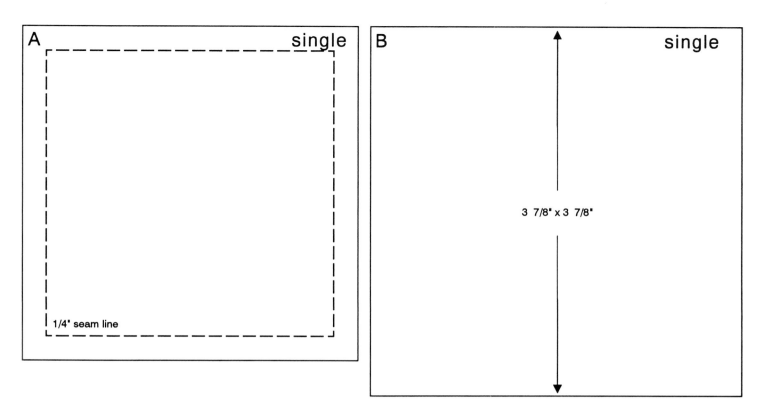

A   single

1/4" seam line

B   single

3 7/8" x 3 7/8"

To construct templates for "edging blocks" and "corner blocks":

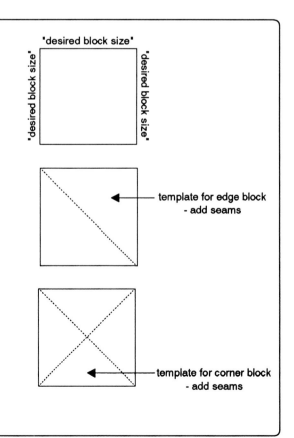

"desired block size"

"desired block size"

"desired block size"

"desired block size"

1   Draw a line the "desired block size" long.
    Crib: 7 1/2"   all other sizes: 15"

2. At the endpoints, draw a line at a 90 degree angle to create square corners. Draw these lines the "desired block size" long. This completes sides two and three of the square.

3. Connect the endpoints of sides two and three. Measure to be sure side four is the correct length and the corners are square.

template for edge block
- add seams

4. To obtain template for "edging blocks", draw a diagonal line, corner to corner, through the square. One of the resulting triangles is your template. Place this diagonal line on the straight of grain when tracing template on fabric. Remember to add seam allowances when cutting fabric.

5. To obtain template for "corner blocks", draw diagonals in both directions, corner to corner, through the square. One of the resulting triangles is your template. Place the edges created by the diagonal lines on the straight grain when tracing template on fabric. Remember to add seam allowances when cutting fabric.

template for corner block
- add seams

Seth Foster

*Seth Foster, George Stearns: The two were to become partners in
an endeavor which would change quilters' lives forever.*

George Stearns

Stitch By Stitch ...
The Texture of Quilting

"The back, being satisfactorily stretched (on the frame), the cotton fill is laid on. The strips of batting should overlap each other about a quarter of an inch and the layers should run in opposite directions. This conceals the joining of the wadding and prevents thin streaks appearing when the quilt is later washed. 'Bat wadding' rather than 'sheet' is preferable, because, having more resiliency, it throws the quilting into greater relief. For ordinary quilts an average of one-half pound to the square yard is used. This amount spreads into two thicknesses over the entire quilt, and, while heavy enough to 'quilt up' well, is still light enough to be easily handled."[1]

When a fellow church member suggested in 1846 that there was a real market for a cotton batting that would not stretch or tear, it is little wonder that George Stearns and Seth Foster were intrigued. Wives of both men were quilters. They were, then, both aware of the lengthy procedure that needed to be followed before quilting could even begin. The enterprising pair, who later called themselves the Stearns and Foster Company (makers of today's Mountain Mist Quilt Batting), began experimenting by spreading a paste of flour and water on a marble slab, rolling a piece of batting on top, and allowing the concoction to dry. The result was a product that was of more uniform thickness, resisted tearing, and had reduced lint.[2]

Prior to mass availability of sheet batting, or cotton wadding as it was called, quilters, in addition to mastering stitching skills, had to be knowledgeable in judging how much wadding was required to show the quilting designs to their best advantage. Too much wadding made quilting difficult to execute and tended to look stuffed. Too little wadding made stitching easier, but resulted in a design that was flat and without texture.

As sheet batting such as that made by Stearns and Foster was not widely available until over 50 years after its development, wadding had to undergo a lengthy preparation procedure before it could even be laid on. Seeds had to be removed to

Cotton batting, very best White Rose quality, 12 oz. roll: price 55¢ per roll: two rolls for $1.00. Sheet wadding, 72" x 90", put up in roll, 95¢. Extra quality bed-puff wool batting, 72" x 90", weight 3 pounds, put up in box, $4.00.

...Ladies' Art Company, St. Louis, Missouri, 1928

White-on-white quilts were often the style of choice as Bridal Quilts of the early 1800's. It is believed that this is one such quilt. Laden with beautiful quilting patterns such as the feathered wreath, the quilt also contains several quilted hearts (one surrounding the letter "T") and interlocking rings. When held to the light, seeds embedded in the cotton batting are visible. While not dated, the number of seeds present, along with the style of quilting (double line quilting was in vogue in white-on-white quilts of the 1800's) lead us to believe the quilt was mid-century. Owned by Jeannette Keyser.

QUILTING DESIGNS FOR ALL PURPOSES

We furnish perforated patterns of all our quilting designs. The patterns are perforated on a very high grade of bond paper, and will last indefinitely. They are transferred to the material by means of stamping powder or stamping wax. It is best to use the powder for stamping articles to be quilted, as any part of the outline not covered by the stitches can be rubbed off with a clean cloth without marring the work.

To stamp with powder, place the pattern on the material with the rough side up and secure so that it will not move; cover a soft cloth or poncet with powder and rub over the pattern. Then remove pattern and a clear outline of the design will be on the material.

Stamping powder, white or blue, 15¢ per box; two boxes for 25¢.

...Ladies' Art Company, date unknown

produce a usable product. Prior to Eli Whitney's cotton gin (1793), seeds were either removed by hand, or with the use of a roller device. Developed in the ancient Orient, this device consisted of two tightly clamped rollers, that when hand-cranked, turned in opposite directions, forcing the cotton between them. While this method did remove many seeds, the wadding still had to be hand-picked to remove additional seeds before it could be easily used. As primitive as the roller device was, it speeded up the output of deseeding cotton from one pound a day by hand to five pounds a day with a roller. Even at this, just preparing the cotton for laying could take anywhere from three to twelve days.[3]

While the invention of the cotton gin revolutionized the cotton industry, it did not completely deseed cotton for the quilter. Some quilts filled with ginned cotton as late as 1850 still contained more seeds than their Southern counterparts that were handpicked.

Contrary to the idea that the presence of cotton seeds dates a quilt to a pre-cotton gin era, seeds did continue to appear in quilts from all parts of the country for generations after the wondrous invention. Perhaps a more reasonable guide to dating a quilt by the presence of seeds was suggested by Ruth Finley when she stated that wadding with a seed or two every few inches suggests a quilt made from 1850 on, while more seeds, say two to three per inch, suggests a date of 1830. As we approach the 21st century, in view of the fragile nature of textiles, it is extremely doubtful that we are likely to come upon a quilt made prior to the cotton gin in other than a museum setting.

In the 1800's, quilting was still a large part of everyday life, not only for bed covers, but also for upholstery and clothing. At a time when four out of every ten children died before the age of six, either in childbirth or due to childhood diseases, quilting was not only a way to provide warmth for your family, it was also a way to work through some of the grief. Quilts were made to line caskets, as well as for keepsakes in a day when photos of loved ones were non-existent.[4]

Women also put their quilting skills to use raising money for causes important to them, be it

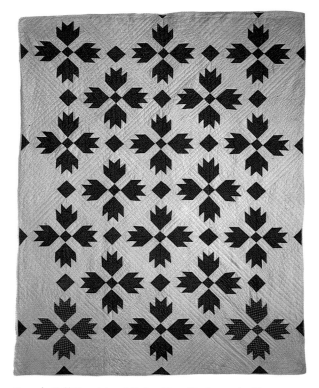

Fannie Bell Parrish, of Cuba, New York, marked her quilting pattern with blue stamping powder when she make her Bear's Paw quilt c. 1850-1870. Still visible along many areas of the quilt (see detail), even more lines can be seen when the quilt is held up to the light. Some of the stamping powder which made the lines so clearly visible for stitching sifted through the fabric to become embedded in the batting beneath. Collection of Dana and Phyllis Scutt.

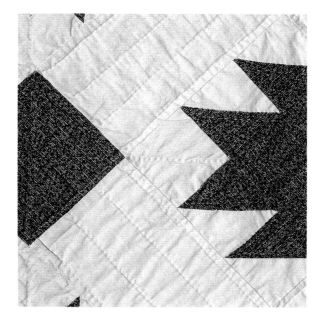

*(2 1/2 meaning 2 1/2 yards, or 90" square)

church, school, or community. Many a church received new carpeting, roofs, organs, and hymnals due to the work of its ladies who did quilting for hire. An 1861 account book records the work of one such church group as follows:

> "Tied and bound comforters, 15¢
> (all material found by the owner)
> Quilting, 1/2" crossbar,
> ordinary size 2 1/2 x 2 1/2*
> fancy feather border...$2.00.
> Marking, 10¢ extra."

Comparative economic values of the day equate this to wages of one cent per hour.[5]

Women used a variety of scales to determine wages for quilting services. Some "quilted on the half," that is, the customer supplied goods for two quilts, one of which the quiltmaker kept in payment for her skills. Some charged by the amount of thread used, as more complex designs would require greater amounts of thread. Until 1850, thread was sold in hanks which were often rewound on thread winders for easier usage. After that time, thread, imported from Scotland, was wound on wooden spools for which the homemaker paid a deposit, which she received back when the empty spool was returned.[6]

Women used a variety of simple tools to enable them to quilt. The frame was made of four strips of lumber, each with fabric attached to them. The backing was pinned to the four bars, taking care to stretch the fabric evenly so as to avoid any areas of uneven tension. Once fastened, the bars were squared up and joined in the corners to hold their position. Held with a peg-and-hole system, clamped, or tied, the frame was then set on legs to keep it at the right height for working. The legs may have been sawhorses, chair backs, or specially constructed legs just for that purpose. In early days, ladderback chairs were developed to meet the need of the quilter. When propped on the uppermost rungs of the ladderback, the frame was a comfortable height to stand at and tie a comforter, with minimal backache. When set on the lower rungs, the frame was the proper height for a seated quilter.

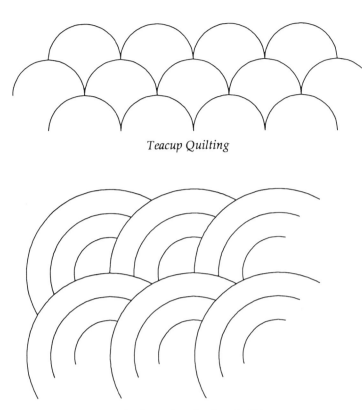

Teacup Quilting

Methodist or Baptist Fan Quilting

Due to the length of time required to complete a quilt, and the great number of quilts needed to outfit a family, the frame almost always had a quilt in it. In small houses that did not have the luxury of a "spare room," a rope and pulley system was set up in which the quilt could be hoisted up to the ceiling when the room was needed for other uses, or lowered when it was time to quilt.

A variety of household goods served as tools and templates when it came time to mark the quilting pattern onto the quilt top. Tea cups were much in favor for creating overlapping circular designs. As early teacups did not have handles, tracing around them was an easy feat.

Another popular quilting pattern, known as Methodist Fan (or Baptist Fan[7], depending on the denomination of the group using the pattern), was a series of concentric overlapping circles marked with a pencil on a string.

In communities where neighbors were nearby, quilting bees became a much-looked-forward-to social event. In colder climates, chores during winter months took on a different flavor. There was no gardening, and as a great deal of food had already been "put up" for the winter, there was more time for indoor activities. Often times, travel was restricted. It was during winter months that many quilt tops were constructed. Come spring and the first sign of good roads, neighbors contacted neighbors, and quilting bees were planned. It was a chance to gather with friends and catch up on the winter's news. Stitching always went faster when you had friends to stitch with. With such large frames, three or four quilters could be seated on each side of the quilt, stitching in as far as they could reach. When that stitching was completed, the corners of the frame were unclamped, the worked section was rolled up, thereby exposing a new section to be quilted, and the corners were reclamped. As the frame got smaller, some of the quilters left the frame to assist in meal preparation, for when the quilt was done, stitchers were rewarded with a picnic feast.

With quilting such an important part of everyday life, it didn't take long for ink manufacturer George Stearns and grocer Seth Foster to recognize the demand for their potential new product.

Calling their first product cotton wadding (essentially the same as batting, but with more compressed fibers) and with a $1500 investment and a few tools, the Stearns and Foster Company was born. Incorporated in 1882, Stearns and Foster became one of Ohio's oldest corporations, and continued to expand. At a time when the style of quilting was changing in America, Stearns and Foster was doing its best to develop a healthy trade. They expanded their wadding business to service other industries: padding for upholstery in automobiles, cotton for surgical and medical needs, and fiber for filtration systems, to name but a few. As mail order sources for quilting supplies sprang up, batting became more universally available.

In 1889, Ladies' Art Company of St. Louis formed. Their first catalog in 1892 offered patterns for piecing, appliqué, and quilting by mail. By 1907, the catalog had been revised at least 10 times, and offered 500 patterns.

Other companies also offered goods to the quilter. The 1890 Montgomery Ward catalog listed cotton fabric for patchwork at 6¢ per yard, with batting ranging from 28¢ to 77¢, depending upon the quality desired. The 1895 - 1896 Sears catalog offered extra wide sheeting in widths of 88", 90", and 104" for quilts with seamless backs. With wool blankets listing from $2.25 to $8.00, it was still less expensive for stitchers to make their own bed coverings.[8]

By 1929, Stearns and Foster put a concerted effort into marketing their batting, and in doing so, piqued the interest of a new generation of quilters. To increase the value of their quilt batting, they printed a quilt pattern inside every wrapper, along with a 15¢ coupon good towards the purchase of any of the dozens of patterns they offered. Merchants were supplied with display ideas designed to increase sales. Quilt shows were sponsored in conjunction with department stores to bring in more customers. Rather than selling under a variety of names as they had in the past (such as Boon, Homestead, Governor, Star, and Cardinal), they chose Mountain Mist as their product name. Fredrich Hooker, head of the batting department, hired quilters to develop patterns they could incorporate onto their labels, and began the quilt collection Mountain Mist has become famous for.

Marketed under the name Mountain Mist, the Stearns and Foster product boasted a free pattern and coupon in every package. Courtesy of Stearns Technical Textiles Company.

With the interest in quilting once again blossoming, newspapers sought to lure a greater female readership. By 1934, more than 400 newspapers ran a quilt pattern column. Quilt shows and contests of the day were attracting thousands, setting records, some of which have yet to be broken. The Detroit News Quilt Show of November 1933 attracted over 50,000 people in three days, while the Century of Progress competition sponsored by Sears and Roebuck, in conjunction with Chicago's 1933 exposition, received 24,878 entries vying for $7,500 prize money.

Ironically, as the interest in quiltmaking rose, the Ladies' Art Company, pioneers in the pattern field, planned to close their doors in May of 1936. World War II changed the lives of American women, many of whom began to work outside the home for the first time. The role of quilting in their lives changed. While some quilting was still being done, mass production finally made it less expensive to buy a blanket than to make one. Families with more income and less time found this an agreeable situation. It wasn't until the approach of our Nation's Bicentennial that quilting began to blossom once again.

Many technological changes have occurred in the way we cut and reshape our fabric. Some prefer time-tested hand sewing methods, while others prefer time-saving machine techniques. Both have a place in our world. One thing that doesn't change is the way we feel about housework, and what we leave behind.

By the early 1930's, Fredrich Hooker, head of Mountain Mist's batting department, began hiring quilters to develop patterns that could be given as premiums to purchasers of their product. Thus began the Mountain Mist Quilt collection, of which Trumpet Vines and Painted Poppies are a part. Courtesy of Stearns Technical Textiles Company.

"If a woman was to see all the dishes that she had to wash before she died, piled up before her in one pile, she'd lie down and die right then and there. I've always had the name o' being a good housekeeper, but when I'm dead and gone ther ain't anybody goin' to think o' the floors I've swept, and the tables I've scrubbed, and the old clothes I've patched, and the stockin's I've darned...but when one of my grandchildren or great-grandchildren sees one o' these quilts, they'll think about Aunt Jane and wherever I am then, I'll know I ain't forgotten."
Aunt Jane of Kentucky
by Eliza Calvert Hall
1898

Straight Line

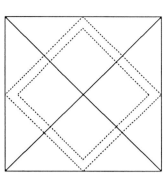
Straight Line

Echo Quilting

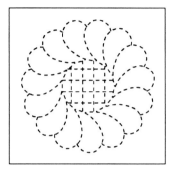
Template Quilting

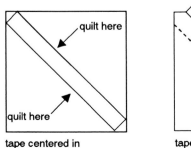
tape centered in
area to be quilted

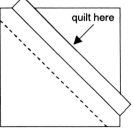
tape repositioned

MARKING YOUR QUILTING PATTERN

Several quilting patterns are given herein for your use. They will add incomparable texture and richness to your quilt. In choosing a quilting pattern, you may want to think of quilting designs in three basic categories:

Straight line: This can either mimic the shape of a pieced pattern, or create a secondary pattern with the use of straight lines.

Echo quilting: Often used in appliqué, echo quilting gets its shape from the motif it is surrounding.

Template quilting: Designs generated from a printed pattern or a stencil.

Straight line quilting not only creates textural designs, but it requires little or no marking on the quilt top to achieve. You can therefore complete the quilt top, sandwich it with batting and backing, and begin quilting. This means that you can, to some extent, let the pattern develop as you work on the quilting itself.

Masking tape is the "marking tool" most often used in straight line quilting. It comes in a variety of widths, and is available in quilting shops, grocery stores, paint stores, etc. If you are quilting 1/4" away from the edge of a pieced pattern, 1/4" wide masking tape is recommended. You can place one edge of the tape even with the seamline, using the other edge as a guide to quilt along. The tape can be removed and repositioned easily as needed, and will hold up well through four or five "re-sticks" before it becomes too linty to adhere well. NEVER leave tape on your quilt when you are not working on it. The adhesive may stain the fabric if it is left on for long periods of time.

Masking tape marking also works well if you are doing parallel lines. Choose a tape whose width equals the distance between your lines. For lines 3/4" apart, for example, position the first length of tape down the center of the area to be covered with parallel lines. Quilt along both edges of the tape. Remove tape, and reposition, aligning one edge of the tape with a line just quilted, and quilt along the other edge, resulting in lines 3/4" apart. By starting

Masking tape can also be used for straight line designs that do not echo a pieced pattern. For example, if you want to quilt a tipped square within a pieced square, measure each side of the pieced square. Stab a straight pin through the quilt at the center of each side. Connect the "dotted midpoints" with strips of masking tape, thereby marking your quilting pattern.

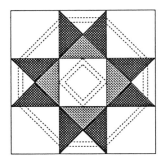

in the center, and working your way to the edges, you will end up with a balanced design, giving you an equal number of lines on each side of the center.

As tape is available in a variety of widths, parallel lines of varying distances can be accommodated.

The only disadvantage I have found with masking tape marking is if you are working with a dark fabric/light batting combination, or a loosely woven fabric. Masking tape can have a tendency to pull fibers of batting up through loosely woven cloth. On dark fabric, this becomes more apparent. Possible solutions would be to use black batting or use echo or template quilting.

Echo quilting, often used around appliqué motifs, also requires no pre-marking on the quilt top itself. The path of the quilting is determined by the shape you are surrounding. The first line of quilting is approximately 1/8" to 1/4" away from the edge of the appliqué motif. This is judged by eye. If you remember that 1/4" is about the width of a pencil, it becomes easier to gauge this distance without marking. If you choose to do an additional row of quilting, it can echo the first line of stitching, again 1/8" - 1/4" away. A third line of quilting would echo the second, etc. As you move farther and farther away from the original motif, the shape formed by the echo tends to soften, much like the outer rings formed when you drop a pebble in a pond.

Do not become concerned if the lines are not precisely parallel over the entire surface of the quilt. Strive for "nearly parallel." There may be spots that will not measure exactly equidistant with a ruler, but if they are nearly parallel, you will achieve the optical illusion of parallel, creating the inviting texture so prevalent in echo quilting.

Template quilting requires that a pattern choice be made before the quilt top is sandwiched, as it is easiest to mark the pattern on the quilt top before it becomes padded with batting. If the pattern source is printed, this is imperative. If the pattern is a stencil, you could mark the top after the layers are sandwiched, although it becomes much more difficult, and may not give satisfactory results.

Once a pattern is chosen, you must next choose the marking tools. Pre-test on scraps of the fabric from your quilt top to be sure the markings will be visible for stitching, and removable after stitching is complete. As felt tip marking pens have a reputation for leaving a chemical residue which can be harmful to the fibers of the quilt, I do not recommend using them. My best results consistently have been with the use of a #3 pencil.

If your pattern is printed, tape the design to a flat surface, then center the quilt top over the design, right side up. Pin the quilt top to the pattern so it doesn't shift as you trace. Using a light hand, trace the pattern onto the cloth, pressing only hard enough so you can see the markings when you are "stitching-distance away" (it isn't necessary to make your lines so dark that you can see them clear across the room).

With any of the illuminated methods (see left), take care when tracing. Trace a short segment, then slip a piece of paper between the quilt top and the pattern to see how dark the marking actually is. You won't need to press as hard as you think for the line to show. The white batting behind the quilt top will make your marking more visible.

If you have difficulty seeing the pattern through the fabric, try one of the following tips:

- *Place white paper under your pattern. This makes the lines of the pattern more visible.*

- *Work where you can place a light source under the pattern. A glass-top coffee table or patio table works well, or fake it by opening your dining room table and place a storm window over the opening. Place a lamp on the floor under the table. TAKE CARE THAT NO FABRIC COMES IN CONTACT WITH THE LAMP WHEN IT IS ON. The lit lamp under the table will illuminate the pattern making it more visible through the fabric.*

- *On a bright day, you can tape the pattern to a window, then top it with the quilt. The light shining through the window will illuminate the pattern so you may trace easily.*

- *When there is no sunlight, try taping the pattern to your television screen. Turn the TV to a station you DON'T get. The bright light from the screen will illuminate the pattern for you.*

When tracing, do not be sketchy with your pencil line. Keep the line as smoothly flowing as possible. This line is your guideline for stitching. If it is sketchy, it will be hard to get smooth alignment when you stitch.

If using a stencil, place the quilt top on a flat surface, right side up. Top with the stencil. You may want to tape the stencil in place so it doesn't slip as you trace. The stencil gives you the design in a perforated format. Trace either along the left edge of the cut-out, the right edge, or the center, as you choose, but be consistent. Watch what you are tracing. It is not necessary to mark the pattern number of the stencil, or the hole that allows the shopowner to display the stencil, or the markings on the stencil which allow you to adjoin it with another pattern. In other words, *don't get so close to the pattern that you can't see what you are tracing!*

Once the pattern has been marked on the quilt top, you are now ready to sandwich the layers of the quilt in preparation for quilting.

Hearts combine with the Sunflower motif to create a quilting pattern for a 12"-15" block.

You may note that I did not discuss quilting-in-the-ditch, a design choice preferred by some quilters. In this method, quilting is done along the seamline, causing the pattern to puff up, without the appearance of the quilting stitch. I prefer not to quilt in this manner for a couple of reasons. If the quilting follows a pieced seam, I feel this puts undue pressure on the piecing stitches that hold the quilt top together, giving way to split seams in the future. The only thing I hate worse than cleaning my oven is mending, and this would mean I would have to mend. The other reason is that I work hard to make my stitches straight and even, and if I am going to go to the effort of quilting, I want my stitches to show.

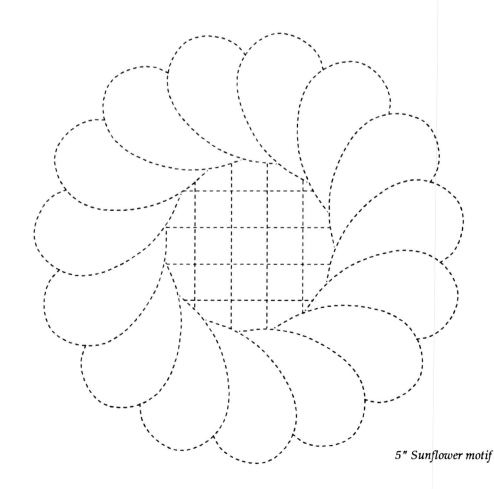

5" Sunflower motif

6" quilted heart

This 6" motif may be used in a variety of
ways to construct larger quilting designs.

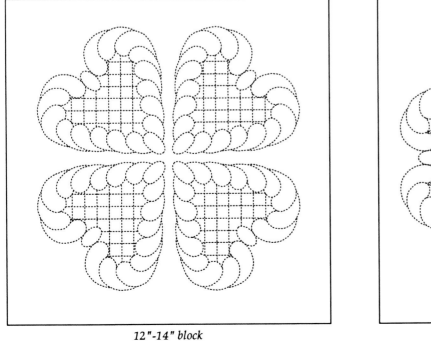

12"-14" block

13"-16" block

8" feathered wreath

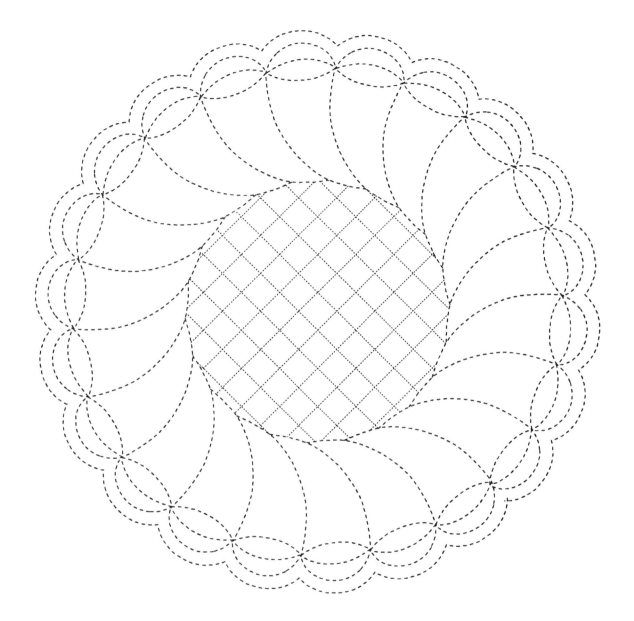

6" feathered wreath

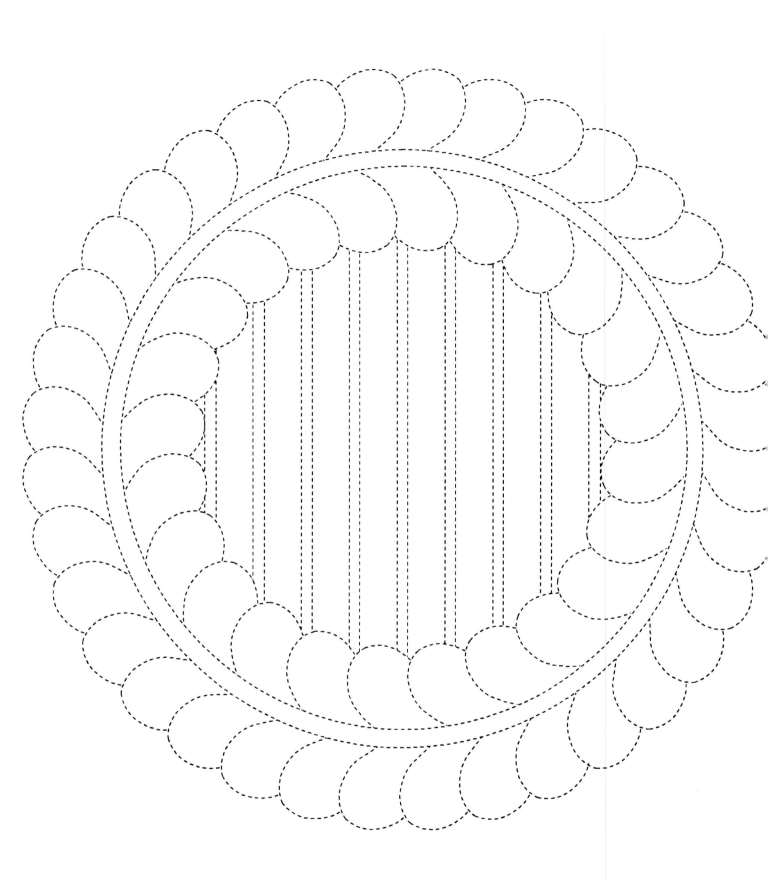

8" corded wreath

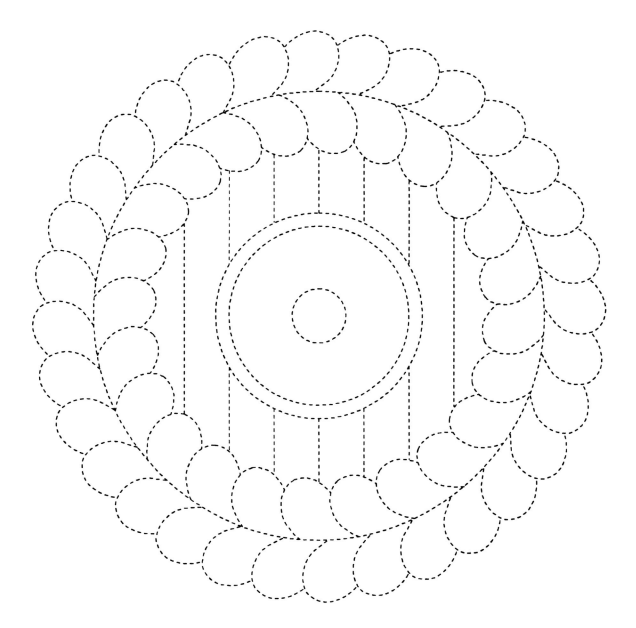

6" wreath within a wreath

8" heart within a heart

Adapted from a cookie mold, this heart-within-a-heart makes a delightful quilting pattern.
~cookie mold designed by Brown Bag Cookie Art~

FINISHING FINESSE

In finishing the edges of a quilt, there are two considerations to keep in mind in order to obtain a quilt that is "square", lays flat, and does not distort on the edges: One consideration is borders that are the proper length, and the other is binding that has not been stretched along the edge.

Fabric is a very "fluid" medium. That is, it stretches and distorts easily. When quilters are ready to add their borders, they often measure along the edge of the quilt to determine the length border they need. The problem with this is that the edges stretch.

To avoid this, measure the quilt top through the center as shown to find the width of the quilt. Measure the same distance on the top and bottom border strips, spacing this measurement evenly around the midpoint.

For example, in calculating 6" wide borders that miter in the corner of a 72" quilt top:

1. Measure the width of the quilt, raw edge to raw edge, through the center of the quilt. (This is usually smaller than the measurement obtained when measuring along the edge of the quilt due to the fact that the edge is stretchier. It hasn't been stabilized by surrounding fabric, therefore it "grows" as you measure it.)

Measuring from raw edge to raw edge automatically builds in seam allowances for you. In our example, this would be 72 1/2".

2. If you plan to miter the corners of the border, ADD to the center measurement two times the border width.

ex: Strips for 6" wide borders would be:
6" +72 1/2" +6" =84 1/2" long* by 6 1/2" wide**

*Since the seam allowance for length was built in on step 1, it's already included in step 2.

**Cutting strips 6 1/2" wide will result in borders finishing to 6" wide.

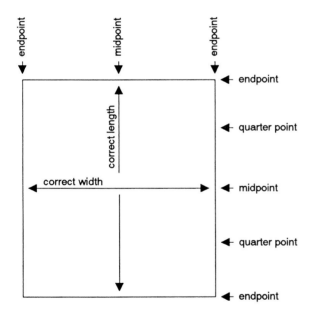

3. On the strip 84 1/2" long, mark the midpoint. Center the 72 1/2" measurement around this, indicating "endpoints" for you. Mark quarter points (midway between the endpoints and the center point).

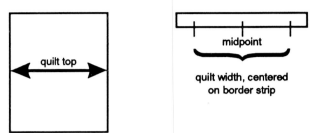

4. Match the midpoint of the top border to the midpoint of the top of the quilt. Match the ends of the quilt top to the pins in step 3 on the top border strip. THERE WILL BE EXCESS BORDER AT BOTH ENDS. Stitch with 1/4" seams, beginning and ending your stitching 1/4" from the raw edge. Repeat with the bottom border strip.

5. To attach the side borders, repeat the procedure, measuring through the center of the quilt lengthwise.

If there is a great deal of excess to be eased in, this is a warning flag that accuracy has been lost somewhere along the way, and construction should be examined and adjusted before borders are added.

Once all 4 border bands have been added in this manner, easing the edge of the quilt where necessary to conform to the "through the center" measurement, you are ready to miter the corners.

TO MITER CORNERS:

1. Position quilt on table so borders lay out open flat. The "tails" will be overlapping in each corner.

NOTE: *If you have built in excess for margin for error, there will be excess borders extending beyond the edges. The excess may now be trimmed off.*

Lockstitching:

A lockstitch is obtained when you either set the stitch length on your machine at 0, so the needle goes up and down, but the fabric doesn't move (thereby knotting it), or by dropping the feed-dogs (the ziggy zaggy things that make the fabric move).

This guarantees that the line of stitching starts and stops exactly where you want it to. The danger with backstitching at this point is that the length of the stitch going forward is not always the same length as that of the stitch going backward, causing you to have a stitch where you don't want it, resulting in a pucker or pleat.

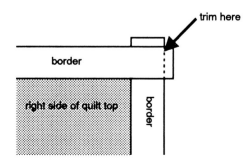

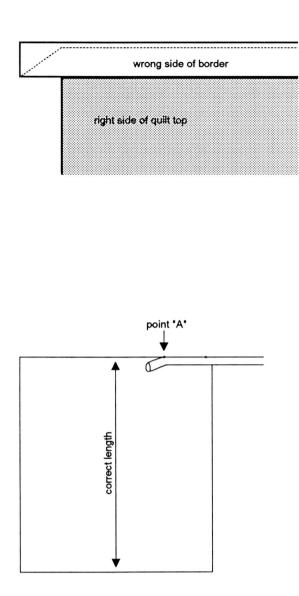

Binding can also distort the edges of a quilt, due primarily to the stretchiness of the bias fabric used. This can cause rippling edges, as well as uneven width of binding.

2. On the wrong side of the border, using a ruler, draw a diagonal line from where your stitching to the quilt top ended to the outside corner of the border. Do this on all 8 tails.

3. In each corner, place the border strips right sides together, and pin, matching the diagonal lines just drawn. Stitch on the line, from where the stitching to the quilt top ended to the outside corner of the border. Open the border out to be sure the miter is correct. Trim off excess fabric, leaving 1/4" seam. Press.

Most quilters, in binding their quilts, begin at point A, work their way around the quilt, and end where they began, applying bias as they go. Uneven stretching of both the quilt's edge and the bias during application can lead to problems.

Ideally, begin at point A, about 4" from a corner. Apply binding up to the corner, position binding for mitering, (see *Edge Finishing* below) then STOP.

Measure how long the next edge is supposed to be (again by measuring through the center of the quilt), measure a corresponding length of bias, being careful not to stretch the bias as you measure, and apply, again matching endpoints, midpoints, quarter points, and easing in between.

Repeating this procedure on all 4 sides results in a quilt that is "square."

EDGE FINISHING

Professional edge finishing can be achieved by mitering the binding of your quilt as you turn the corners.

1. For a 1/4" bound edge, cut bias strips of cloth 2" wide (see *Continuous Bias with a Rotary Cutter* on page 104). Fold in half, wrong sides together, edges even. Press.

2. Pin folded bias to the edge you are binding, all raw edges even, starting about 4" from a corner. Begin stitching about 2" from the beginning of the bias, using a 1/4" seam, stitching through all layers.

3. To miter corners, stop stitching 1/4" from the end of the quilt. Lockstitch at this point.

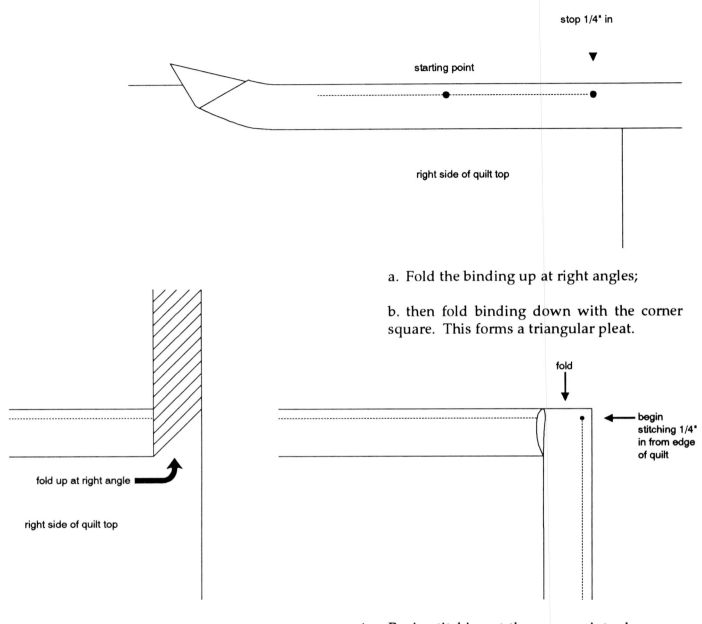

stop 1/4" in

starting point

right side of quilt top

a. Fold the binding up at right angles;

b. then fold binding down with the corner square. This forms a triangular pleat.

fold

begin stitching 1/4" in from edge of quilt

fold up at right angle

right side of quilt top

4. Begin stitching at the same point where you ended your previous stitching with a lockstitch. Continue stitching to the next corner. Repeat mitering procedure.

5. Ending binding: Stop stitching about 4" from the starting point. Remove piece from the machine. On the unstitched portion of the "beginning", turn under 1/2". (This edge will be angled, as the strip was cut on the bias. This is correct.)

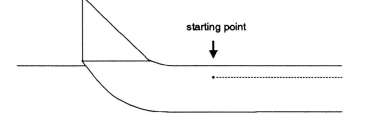

starting point

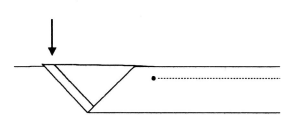

6. Cut the tail of the binding so it extends 1/2" past the fold. Tuck the excess tail inside the folded "beginning." Stitch the remaining binding in place. This results in an angled seam at the joint, thereby distributing the bulk of the seam and avoiding lumps.

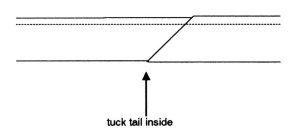

tuck tail inside

7. Pull the binding up over the seam, encasing it. The fold on the edge of the bias will just cover the machine stitching that holds the binding to the quilt. Blindstitch in place.

8. In the corners, fold binding to encase one edge first. This miters the binding on the front of the quilt.

9. Now fold binding to encase the second edge. This miters the binding on the back of the quilt. Blindstitch the miter folds on the front and the back of the quilt.

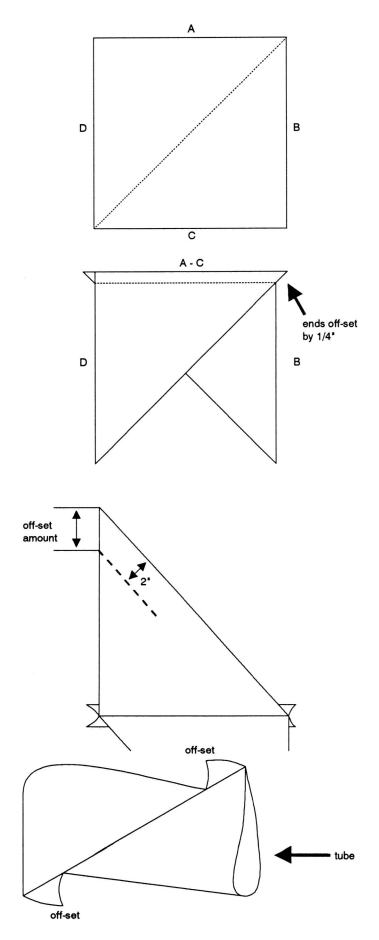

1. Cut a square of cloth. Cut in half on the diagonal. Label sides as shown.

2. Match the top (A) and bottom (C) edges of the square, off-setting the ends 1/4" as shown, and stitch with a 1/4" seam. Press seam OPEN to reduce bulk. Lay fabric out flat.

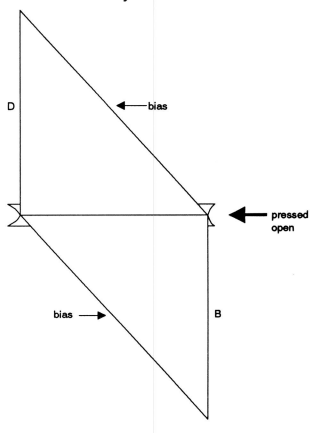

3. Decide on the width of your bias strip. For 1/4" wide finished edging, I recommend 2". Measure 2" in from one of the BIAS edges, as shown by the dotted line. The "straight grain edge" of the 2" strip, from the dotted line to the corner, will be the "off-set" amount in the next step.

4. Place sides B and D right sides together, off-setting the amount achieved in Step 3. (If it looks twisted and crooked, like you did something wrong, you've done it right!) Stitch with a 1/4" seam. Press seam open. A tube has been formed. Turn tube right side out.

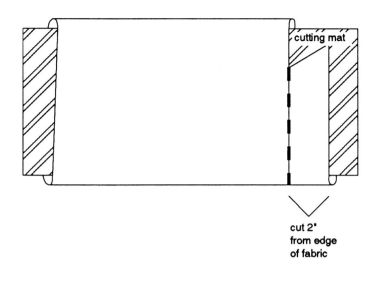

cutting mat

cut 2"
from edge
of fabric

5. Insert a cutting mat into the tube. Position a cutting ruler (Quickline®, Salem® etc.) so the 2" mark of the ruler aligns with the bias edge of the tube, and 2" of ruler covers the fabric. Cut along this edge with a rotary cutter.

NOTE: YOU MAY ONLY CUT THROUGH ONE LAYER AT A TIME FOR THIS TO WORK!!!

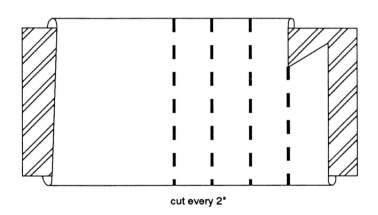

cut every 2"

6. Reposition the ruler so the 2" marking aligns with the cut just made, and 2" of ruler covers a new section of the tube. Cut. Repeat until the entire exposed surface has been cut every 2".

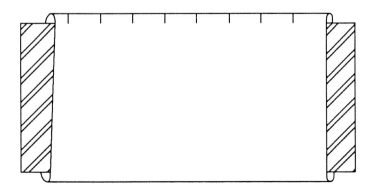

7. Reposition the tube on the mat so an uncut expanse is exposed, leaving about 1" of slashes showing. Repeat above cutting procedure, connecting "old cuts" with "new cuts."

8. Depending on the size of your tube and your mat, you may need to reposition your tube three or four times to connect the slashes. The entire tube has now been cut and can be wound off the board.

Checklist for a well-finished quilt:

- *Finished quilt should be the same width on the edges that it is through the center.*

- *Finished quilt should be the same length on the edges that it is through the center.*

- *Binding should be of uniform width.*

- *Application stitches on binding should be invisible.*

- *All four corners should be treated the same (i.e. rounded in all four, mitered in all four, etc.)*

- *Binding mitered in the corners should be mitered on both the front and the back, and stitched along the miter on both the front and the back.*

- *The seam at the joint (where the binding's beginning and ending meet) should be blindstitched.*

- *Binding should be well filled (ex: not lumpy in corners, not skimpy along edges. Batting should extend completely into the binding.*

TO FIGURE YARDAGE FOR MAKING CONTINUOUS BIAS BINDING:

1. To find HOW LARGE A SQUARE TO START WITH for the amount of bias you need, multiply the length (in inches) of bias you need by the width you plan to cut the bias, and find the square root. (Most pocket calculators have a square root function button on them, so this is really easy to do.) This will give you the size square you need to start with.

Example: for a quilt that finishes to 48" x 48":

a. 48" x 4 = 192" (amount of bias needed)
b. 192" x 2" (cut 2" wide binding) = 384 square inches
c. The square root of 384 is 19.59

Start with a square 20" to 21" to give yourself a margin for error.

2. If you want to know HOW MUCH BIAS WILL A SQUARE YIELD, multiply the length of the square by the width, and divide the result by the width of bias you are cutting.

Example: for a 20" square:

a. 20" x 20" = 400 square inches
b. 400" divided by 2 = 200" of bias tape (plenty for our 48" square quilt)

"You will never 'find' time for anything.
If you want time, you must make it."

Charles Buxton
from "The Quiltie Ladies' Scrapbook"[1]

REFERENCE LIST

SURVIVAL BY ANY MEANS... LOG CABINS AND SODDIES

1. *Quilters' Journal*, Spring 1979, Vol. 2, No. 1, p. 18. Joyce Gross, Editor/Publisher, P.O. Box 270, Mill Valley, California 94941

2. Quoted in *Hearts and Hands*, Ferrero, et al., p. 56, from Roger L. Welsch's *Sod Walls: The Story of the Nebraska Sod House*, p. 88, Purcells, Inc., Broken Bow, Nebraska, 1968

3. *American Patchwork Quilt*, p. 23, Spencer Museum of Art, The University of Kansas, 1987

4. This is one of sixty to seventy quilts in the Chemung County Historical Society collection.

5. Frost, S. Annie, *Ladies Guide to Needle Work, Embroidery, Etc.*, 1877; unabridged reproduction of the original which was first published in 1877, 1986 by R. L. Shep, Mendocino, California

6. It is interesting to note that a hint which amazes students today regarding how to properly thread a needle so as to prevent tangling was presented in this 1869 *Guide to Women in How To Keep a Home*.

A SCHOOLHOUSE REVISITED

1. Compiled from recollections of teachers from the 1872 time period, this list of rules is made available to visitors of one of the Nation's oldest schoolhouses, the Oldest Wooden Schoolhouse Museum in St. Augustine, Florida. When questioned about the oddity of some of the rules, it was explained that many schools fired young women once they married (item #6), believing that their job once married was to stay home and care for their own children. In reference to item #8, to visit a barber was considered an extravagance. Teachers were expected to cut their own hair, thereby saving money. In addition, barber shops were often in close proximity to pool halls and women of questionable honor. To be seen frequenting such a place meant certain dismissal.

2. Finley, Ruth, *Old Patchwork Quilts and The Women Who Made Them*, Charles T. Branford Co., Newton Centre, Massachusetts, 1929, reprinted 1970, pp. 57-78

3. *Primary Manual Training*, Caroline F. Cutler, 1892, p. 73

4. As displayed at the Buffalo and Erie County Historical Society, Buffalo, New York, January-February, 1991

5. The first sewing machine was patented in 1790 by Englishman Thomas Saint. Another was patented in 1830 by Frenchman Barthélemy Thimonnier. Designed to sew soldiers' uniforms, Thimonnier's invention was the cause of an angry mob scene, as workers wrecked his machines because they put so many men out of work.

6. Barbara Brackman, renowned historian of quilt patterns and their origins, has documented the appearance of the schoolhouse as a patchwork pattern in *Clues in the Calico*, p. 170.

THE WILDERNESS AROUND US... THE BEAR'S PAW

1. The Ladies' Art Company (LAC) of St. Louis, Missouri, founded in 1889, was a mail order company which was the first to attempt to collect quilt patterns and associate them with the name they were known by at that time. Prior to this, while patterns did appear occasionally in magazines, almanacs, etc., they were unnamed, and appeared merely as a drawing of the finished design, without directions or templates. The LAC catalogs, first known as *Diagrams of Quilt, Sofa and Pin Cushion Patterns*, later became *Quilt Patterns: Patchwork and Applique*. By 1898, 420 patterns were offered, increasing by 1928 to 530 patterns.

2. Averil Colby's book *Patchwork* made reference to the sawtoothing form of quilt embellishment on pp. 47-48.

3. The 1990 *Figurative Quilts and Bedcovers 1700-1900* exhibit held at the Los Angeles County Museum of Art, curated by Sandi Fox, made the correlation between clothing embellishment and quiltmaking techniques in the book which chronicles the exhibit, *Wrapped in Glory*.

THE ROSE... A FLOWER OF HOPES AND DREAMS

1. Crowell, Robert, *The Lore and Legends of Flowers*, Crowell Press, New York, 1982

2. Catharine E. Beecher was a leader in the reform for equal education for women. A firm believer that women were just as capable of learning as men, Ms. Beecher was instrumental in the founding of women's academies for the higher education of women. With her sister, Harriet Beecher Stowe (of *Uncle Tom's Cabin* fame), she co-authored *The American Woman's Home: A Guide to Women in How To Keep a Home*. Feeling women were woefully unprepared for the immensity of the role of housewife, she offered advice on everything from how to build a fire, to how to efficiently arrange the household, to how to properly make a bed.

p. 359, "The best beds are thick hair mattresses, which for persons in health are good for winter as well as summer use. Mattresses may also be made of husks, dried and drawn into shreds; also of alternate layers of cotton and moss. All bed-linen should be marked and numbered, so that a bed can always be made properly, and all missing articles be known."

p. 370, "The following directions should be given to those who do this work: (making a bed)

Open the windows, and lay off the bed-covering on two chairs, at the foot of the bed. If it be a feather-bed, after it is well aired, shake the feathers from each corner to the middle; then take up the middle, shake it well, and turn the bed over. Then push the feathers in place, making the head higher than the foot, and the sides even, and as high as the middle part. A mattress, whether used on top of a feather-bed or by itself, should in like manner be well aired and turned. Then put on the bolster and the under sheet, so that the wrong side of the sheet shall go next the bed, and the markings always come at the head, tucking in all around. Then put on the pillows, evenly, so that the open ends shall come to the sides of the bed, and spread on the upper sheet so that the wrong side shall be next to the blankets, and the marked end always at the head. This arrangement of sheets is to prevent the part where the feet lie from being reversed, so as to come to the face; and also to prevent the parts soiled by the body from coming to the bedtick and blankets. Put on the other covering, except the outer one, tucking in all around, and then turn over the upper sheet at the head, so as to show a part of the pillows. When the pillow-cases are clean and smooth, they look best outside of the cover, but not otherwise. Then draw the hand along the side of the pillows, to make an even indentation, and then smooth and shape the whole outside. A nice housekeeper always notices the manner in which a bed is made; and in some parts of the country, it is rare to see this work properly performed."

3. *Old Quilts* by William Rush Dunton, Jr., M.D., published by the author, Catonsville, Maryland, 1946, p. 18. Dr. Dunton, a psychiatrist and a founding father of occupational therapy, is better remembered today as an ardent fan of the Baltimore Album Quilt. Perhaps the first to study the genre in depth, his work is the foundation for much of what we now know about the quilts peculiar to the mid-1800's Baltimore area. Firmly believing that the occupation of quiltmaking would be beneficial to those under his care, he carefully collected both fact and lore about the needleart that so captured his imagination, the story about the cat being one such tidbit of information.

THE APPLIQUÉ OF NATURE... STAR AND TULIP QUILT

1. florin - a gold coin first made in Florence in the 1200's. It bore the imprint of a lily on one side and the figure of Saint John the Baptist on the other side. The word "florin" comes from the Latin word for flower. Florins, or guilders, are used now in the Netherlands.

2. Coats, Alice, *Flowers and Their Histories*, p. 255

Hand dyed and marbleized fabrics from New York Beauty Dye Works, Sheryll Robbins, 604 N. Madison Street, Rome, New York 13440, 315-337-2363

YOUNG MAN'S FANCY... OR GOOSE IN THE POND

1. Brackman, Barbara, *Clues in the Calico*

2. Finley, Ruth, *Old Patchwork Quilts and The Women Who Made Them*, p. 83

3. Ruby McKim, *One Hundred and One Patchwork Patterns*, p. 35

STITCH BY STITCH... THE TEXTURE OF QUILTING

1. Ruth Finley, *Old Patchwork Quilts and The Women Who Made Them*, p. 46

2. From information provided by The Stearns Technical Textiles Company, makers of Mountain Mist Quilt Batting

3. Ruth Finley, op. cit., p. 134.

4. Quilt Digest I, p. 53, "The Reiter Quilt: A Family Story in Cloth," by Julie Silber

5. Ruth Finley, op. cit., p. 94. Mrs. Finley recounts in her landmark book the finding, in a box of trash, of a partial record of the quilting done by the members of a parish's Dorcas Society. Prices for services rendered in 1861, when compared to the value on household goods of the day, equated to but pennies a day in 1929.

6. Averil Mathis, "Thimbles, Thimble Holders and Thread Winders," *American Quilters Society* magazine, Summer 1986, p. 15

7. *American Patchwork Quilts*, p. 30

8. Barbara Brackman, *Clues in the Calico*, p. 26

9. Written in 1898, *Aunt Jane of Kentucky*, by Eliza Calvert Hall, chronicles the life of "Aunt Jane," a delightfully outspoken character liable to launch into the spinning of a tale on a moment's notice. Most recently reprinted in 1985, this book captures a homespun warmth in the best style of storytelling.

FINISHING FINESSE

1. *The Quiltie Ladies' Scrapbook*, by Variable Star Quilters, Souderton, Pennsylvania, 1987

Quilted Heart inspired by cookie mold from Brown Bag Cookie Art, by Hill Design
77 Regional Drive
Concord, New Hampshire 03301
1-800-228-4488

Background on the development of Stearns and Foster Company courtesy of The Stearns Technical Textiles Company, Consumer Products Division, 100 Williams Street, Cincinnati, Ohio

MUSEUMS

Buffalo and Erie County Historical Society, 25 Nottingham Court, Buffalo, New York 14216

Chemung County Historical Society, 415 East Water Street, Elmira, New York 14901

Horseheads Historical Society, Grand Central Avenue, Horseheads, New York 14845

Nebraska State Historical Society, P.O. Box 82554, 1500 R Street, Lincoln, Nebraska 68501

Oldest Wooden Schoolhouse Museum, St. Augustine, Florida

Winterthur Museum, Winterthur, Delaware 19735

BIBLIOGRAPHY

Beecher, Catharine E., and Harriet Beecher Stowe, *The American Woman's Home: A Guide to Women in How To Keep a Home,* 1869

Benberry, Cuesta, "An Historic Quilt Document: The Ladies Art Company Catalog," *Quilters' Journal,* Summer 1978, Vol. 1, No. 4, pp. 13-14, Mill Valley, California

Beyer, Jinny, *The Quilter's Album of Blocks and Borders,* EPM Publishing, McLean, Virginia, 1980

Brackman, Barbara, *Clues in the Calico,* EPM Publications, Inc., McLean, Virginia, 1989

Brackman, Barbara, "Patterns to Ponder," *Quilt World Omnibook,* Winter, 1983

Child, Lydia Maria, *The American Frugal Housewife,* 31st edition, 1845

Coats, Alice, *Flowers and Their Histories,* Pitman Publishing Corporation, New York, 1956

Coats, Peter, *Flowers in History,* Viking Press, New York, 1970

Colby, Averil, *Patchwork,* Charles T. Branford, Newton Centre, Massachusetts, 1985

Conrad, Pam, *Prairie Visions: The Life and Times of Solomon Butcher,* HarperCollins Publishers, New York, 1991

Cozart, Dorothy, "A Century of Fund-raising Quilts: 1860-1960," *Uncoverings 1984,* American Quilt Study Group, 1985

Crowell, Robert, *The Lore and Legends of Flowers,* Crowell Press, New York, 1982

Cutler, Caroline F., *Primary Manual Training,* 1892

Dunton, Dr. William Rush Jr., *Old Quilts,* Published by the author, Catonsville, Maryland, 1946

Ferrero, Pat, Elaine Hedges, and Julie Silber, *Hearts and Hands: The Influence of Women & Quilts on American Society,* The Quilt Digest Press, San Francisco, 1987

Finley, Ruth, *Old Patchwork Quilts and the Women Who Made Them,* Lippincott, Philadelphia, 1929; reprinted by C. T. Branford Company, Newton Centre, Massachusetts, 1983

Fox, Sandi, *19th Century American Patchwork Quilt,* The Seibu Museum of Art, Tokyo, Japan, 1983-84

Fox, Sandi, *Wrapped in Glory: Figurative Quilts and Bedcovers 1700-1900,* Thames and Hudson, Los Angeles County Museum of Art, 1990

Frost, S. Annie, *Ladies Guide to Needle Work, Embroidery, Etc.,* 1877, unabridged reproduction of the original which was first published in 1877, copyright 1986 by R. L. Shep, Mendocino, California

Gross, Joyce, Editor/Publisher, *Quilters' Journal,* Spring 1979, Vol. 2, No. 1, p. 18, P.O. Box 270, Mill Valley, California 94941

Hall, Carrie A., and Rose G. Kretsinger, *The Romance of the Patchwork Quilt in America,* Crown Publishers, Inc., New York, 1935

Hall, Eliza Calvert, *Aunt Jane of Kentucky,* R and E Miles, Box 1916, San Pedro, California 90733, reprinted 1985

Ickis, Marguerite, *The Standard Book of Quilt Making and Collecting,* Dover Publications, Inc., New York, 1949

Ladies' Art Company, St. Louis, Missouri, 1928

Lipsett, Linda Otto, *Remember Me: Women and Their Friendship Quilts,* Quilt Digest Press, San Francisco, 1985

Martin, Nancy, *Pieces of the Past,* That Patchwork Place, Bothell, Washington, 1986

Mathis, Averil, "Thimbles, Thimble Holders and Thread Winders," *American Quilters Society* magazine, Summer 1986

McKim, Ruby Short, *One Hundred and One Patchwork Patterns,* Dover Publications, Inc., New York, 1962

Orlofsky, Patsy and Myron, *Quilts in America,* McGraw-Hill Book Company, New York, 1974

Rounds, Glen, *The Treeless Plains,* Holiday House, New York, 1967

Sienkiewicz, Elly, *Spoken Without a Word,* Turtle Hill Press, Washington, D.C., 1983

Sienkiewicz, Elly, *Baltimore Beauties and Beyond, Vol. II,* C & T Publishing, Lafayette, California, 1991

Snyder, Grace, *No Time on My Hands,* University of Nebraska Press, Lincoln and London, 1986

American Patchwork Quilt, p. 23, Spencer Museum of Art, The University of Kansas, 1987

Stratton, Joanna L., *Pioneer Women: Voices from the Kansas Frontier*

Variable Star Quilters, *The Quiltie Ladies' Scrapbook,* Souderton, Pennsylvania, 1987